IF LOST, PLEASE RETU

MW00876052

_____

PHONE: _____

EMAIL: _____

ADDRESS: _____

_____

IN CASE OF EMERGENCY, PLEASE CONTACT:

NAME: _____

PHONE: _____

NAME: _____

PHONE: _____

NAME: _____

PHONE: _____

Thanks for choosing The Ultimate Hiking Logbook!
You're holding an amazing utilitarian-style tool for your hiking adventures. We, as adventurers ourselves, wanted to produce something that would actually be useful for other adventure-seekers.

Our goal was to create a place where you can record all of your great (and sometimes not so great) notes & impressions of your hiking trips.

Here's how to use this book:
1. Use the checklist: Turn to these pages before you ever start packing! Walk through the list & ensure you have everything you need for each awesome adventure. We've included ten checklist pages to get you started.

2. Our Logging System: It's so simple! Just start writing. We made quick checkboxes for many of the everyday items you might want to record for a hike. But, of course we also left space for extra notes of observances, difficulties, route options, etc.

3. Filled up the book? When this one is filled, simply reorder! Or, get a new one each year so you can clearly keep your hikes organized by year for reference later. Just search The Ultimate Hiking Logbook on Amazon and choose yours. Search using the ISBN number of this book to help you locate it again quickly. There are also multiple cover designs to choose from! Be sure to select one by "Nomadic Souls Gear & Apparel".

We hope you love this logbook!
Brandon & Brit Cave
Nomadic Souls Gear & Apparel

THE TEN ESSENTIALS:

Packing the "Ten Essentials" whenever you step out for a hike, even day hikes, is a good habit. On a routine outing you may use only a handful of them or possibly none at all. But when something goes wrong, it is in that moment that you'll really appreciate carrying these 10 items and how they could be essential to your survival.

The original list was assembled in the 1930s by The Mountaineers, a Seattle-based organization for climbers and adventurers, to help hikers prepare for emergencies in the outdoors. Back then, the list included: A map, compass, sunglasses and sunscreen, extra clothing, headlamp/flashlight, first-aid supplies, fire starter, matches, knife and extra food.

Over the years, the list has evolved to a "systems" approach rather than including individual items.

Here's what today's Ten Essentials List looks like:
1. Navigation: map, compass, altimeter, GPS device, personal locator beacon (PLB) or satellite messenger
2. Headlamp/Flashlight (Plus extra batteries)
3. Sun protection: Sunglasses, sun-protective clothes & sunscreen
4. First aid: Including foot care & insect repellent
5. Knife: Plus small tools or gear repair
6. Fire: Matches, lighter, tinder and/or stove
7. Shelter: Carried at all times
8. Extra food: Beyond what you expect
9. Extra water: Beyond what you expect
10. Extra clothes: Beyond what you expect

The exact items from each system that you take should be tailored to the trip you're taking. For example, on a short day hike that's easy to navigate you might choose to take a map, compass and PLB, but leave the GPS and altimeter at home.

On a technical, more complex outing, you might decide you want all those tools to help you find your way. When deciding what to bring, consider factors like weather, terrain, difficulty, duration, & location, especially your distance from help.

On the next few pages, we provide you with quick, light checklists of some of the most common items needed. This is not an exhaustive list and does not include items for overnight hikes. Our focus was to provide a quick list for the average hiker. We encourage you to develop your own list as your hiking style develops.

HIKING TERMS

In the back of the logbook, we've provided a great list of some of the most common hiking terms loosely explained in terms for the average hiker. Many thanks to our friend Hartley Brody for providing us this list. If you'd like more information about hiking written for the everyday hiker, we encourage you to check out Hartley's blog at: www.adventures.hartleybrody.com

PRE-HIKE BASIC CHECKLIST

CLOTHING/FOOTWEAR

[ ] MOISTURE-WICKING UNDERWEAR
[ ] MOISTURE-WICKING SHIRT/PANTS/SHORTS
[ ] BOOTS/SHOES FOR TERRAIN
[ ] SOCKS (SYNTHETIC OR WOOL)
[ ] EXTRA CLOTHING
[ ] LONG-SLEEVE SHIRTS (FOR SUN AND BUGS)

ADDITIONAL ITEMS FOR RAINY AND/OR COLD WEATHER:
[ ] RAINWEAR (JACKET & PANTS)
[ ] LONG UNDERWEAR
[ ] WARM INSULATED JACKET/VEST
[ ] GLOVES
[ ] WARM HAT
[ ] BANDANA OR BUF
[ ] SANDALS (FOR STREAMS AND/OR CAMP SHOES)

HEALTH & HYGIENE

[ ] HAND SANITIZER
[ ] MENSTRUAL PRODUCTS
[ ] PRESCRIPTION MEDICATIONS
[ ] PRESCRIPTION GLASSES
[ ] INSECT REPELLENT
[ ] BLISTER TREATMENT SUPPLIES
[ ] SANITATION TROWEL
[ ] TOILET PAPER/WIPES AND SEALABLE BAG (TO PACK IT OUT)

SUN PROTECTION:
[ ] SUNGLASSES (+ RETAINER LEASH)
[ ] SUNSCREEN
[ ] SPF-RATED LIP BALM
[ ] SUN HAT

TOOLS & REPAIR

[ ] KNIFE OR MULTI-TOOL
[ ] DUCT TAPE

NAVIGATION

[ ] MAP (IN WATERPROOF SLEEVE)
[ ] COMPASS
[ ] ROUTE MAP/GUIDE
[ ] ALTIMETER WATCH
[ ] GPS
[ ] SATELLITE MSSGR/LOCATOR BEACON

BACKPACKING

[ ] BACKPACK
[ ] HEADLAMP/FLASHLIGHT
[ ] TREKKING POLES
[ ] PACKABLE LANTERN
[ ] BEAR SPRAY

FOOD & WATER

[ ] WATER BOTTLES AND/OR RESERVOIR
[ ] WATER FILTER/PURIFIER OR TREATMEN
[ ] FOOD/SNACKS (BARS, CHEWS, TRAIL MIX, DRINK MIX)

EMERGENCY ITEMS

[ ] FIRST-AID KIT OR SUPPLIES
[ ] WHISTLE
[ ] LIGHTER/MATCHES (WATERPROOF)
[ ] FIRE STARTER (FOR SURVIVAL FIRE)
[ ] EMERGENCY SHELTER
[ ] TWO ITINERARIES:
   1 LEFT WITH FRIEND + 1 UNDER CAR SEAT

EXTRAS

[ ] CAMERA (EXTRA MEMORY CARDS)
[ ] INTERPRETIVE FIELD GUIDE(S)
[ ] JOURNAL/SKETCHBOOK & PEN/PENCIL
[ ] COMPACT BINOCULARS
[ ] TWO-WAY RADIOS

PERSONAL ITEMS

[ ] PERMITS (IF NEEDED)
[ ] CREDIT CARD AND/OR CASH ID
[ ] CAR KEYS
[ ] CELL PHONE

PRE-HIKE BASIC CHECKLIST

CLOTHING/FOOTWEAR

[ ] MOISTURE-WICKING
UNDERWEAR
[ ] MOISTURE-WICKING
SHIRT/PANTS/SHORTS
[ ] BOOTS/SHOES FOR TERRAIN
[ ] SOCKS (SYNTHETIC OR WOOL)
[ ] EXTRA CLOTHING
[ ] LONG-SLEEVE SHIRTS
(FOR SUN AND BUGS)

*ADDITIONAL ITEMS FOR RAINY
AND/OR COLD WEATHER:*
[ ] RAINWEAR (JACKET & PANTS)
[ ] LONG UNDERWEAR
[ ] WARM INSULATED JACKET/VEST
[ ] GLOVES
[ ] WARM HAT
[ ] BANDANA OR BUF
[ ] SANDALS (FOR STREAMS AND/OR
CAMP SHOES)

HEALTH & HYGIENE

[ ] HAND SANITIZER
[ ] MENSTRUAL PRODUCTS
[ ] PRESCRIPTION MEDICATIONS
[ ] PRESCRIPTION GLASSES
[ ] INSECT REPELLENT
[ ] BLISTER TREATMENT SUPPLIES
[ ] SANITATION TROWEL
[ ] TOILET PAPER/WIPES AND
SEALABLE BAG (TO PACK IT OUT)

SUN PROTECTION:
[ ] SUNGLASSES (+ RETAINER LEASH)
[ ] SUNSCREEN
[ ] SPF-RATED LIP BALM
[ ] SUN HAT

TOOLS & REPAIR

[ ] KNIFE OR MULTI-TOOL
[ ] DUCT TAPE

NAVIGATION

[ ] MAP (IN WATERPROOF SLEEVE)
[ ] COMPASS
[ ] ROUTE MAP/GUIDE
[ ] ALTIMETER WATCH
[ ] GPS
[ ] SATELLITE MESSENGER/LOCATOR BEACON

BACKPACKING

[ ] BACKPACK
[ ] HEADLAMP/FLASHLIGHT
[ ] TREKKING POLES
[ ] PACKABLE LANTERN
[ ] BEAR SPRAY

FOOD & WATER

[ ] WATER BOTTLES AND/OR RESERVOIR
[ ] WATER FILTER/PURIFIER OR TREATMENT
[ ] FOOD/SNACKS (BARS, CHEWS, TRAIL
MIX, DRINK MIX)

EMERGENCY ITEMS

[ ] FIRST-AID KIT OR SUPPLIES
[ ] WHISTLE
[ ] LIGHTER/MATCHES (WATERPROOF)
[ ] FIRE STARTER (FOR SURVIVAL FIRE)
[ ] EMERGENCY SHELTER
[ ] TWO ITINERARIES:
1 LEFT WITH FRIEND + 1 UNDER CAR SEAT

EXTRAS

[ ] CAMERA (EXTRA MEMORY CARDS)
[ ] INTERPRETIVE FIELD GUIDE(S)
[ ] JOURNAL/SKETCHBOOK & PEN/PENCIL
[ ] COMPACT BINOCULARS
[ ] TWO-WAY RADIOS

PERSONAL ITEMS

[ ] PERMITS (IF NEEDED)
[ ] CREDIT CARD AND/OR CASH ID
[ ] CAR KEYS
[ ] CELL PHONE

PRE-HIKE BASIC CHECKLIST

CLOTHING/FOOTWEAR

[ ] MOISTURE-WICKING
      UNDERWEAR
[ ] MOISTURE-WICKING
      SHIRT/PANTS/SHORTS
[ ] BOOTS/SHOES FOR TERRAIN
[ ] SOCKS (SYNTHETIC OR WOOL)
[ ] EXTRA CLOTHING
[ ] LONG-SLEEVE SHIRTS
      (FOR SUN AND BUGS)

*ADDITIONAL ITEMS FOR RAINY
AND/OR COLD WEATHER:*
[ ] RAINWEAR (JACKET & PANTS)
[ ] LONG UNDERWEAR
[ ] WARM INSULATED JACKET/VEST
[ ] GLOVES
[ ] WARM HAT
[ ] BANDANA OR BUF
[ ] SANDALS (FOR STREAMS AND/OR
      CAMP SHOES)

HEALTH & HYGIENE

[ ] HAND SANITIZER
[ ] MENSTRUAL PRODUCTS
[ ] PRESCRIPTION MEDICATIONS
[ ] PRESCRIPTION GLASSES
[ ] INSECT REPELLENT
[ ] BLISTER TREATMENT SUPPLIES
[ ] SANITATION TROWEL
[ ] TOILET PAPER/WIPES AND
      SEALABLE BAG (TO PACK IT OUT)

SUN PROTECTION:
[ ] SUNGLASSES (+ RETAINER LEASH)
[ ] SUNSCREEN
[ ] SPF-RATED LIP BALM
[ ] SUN HAT

TOOLS & REPAIR

[ ] KNIFE OR MULTI-TOOL
[ ] DUCT TAPE

NAVIGATION

[ ] MAP (IN WATERPROOF SLEEVE)
[ ] COMPASS
[ ] ROUTE MAP/GUIDE
[ ] ALTIMETER WATCH
[ ] GPS
[ ] SATELLITE MSSGR/LOCATOR BEACO

BACKPACKING

[ ] BACKPACK
[ ] HEADLAMP/FLASHLIGHT
[ ] TREKKING POLES
[ ] PACKABLE LANTERN
[ ] BEAR SPRAY

FOOD & WATER

[ ] WATER BOTTLES AND/OR RESERVOI
[ ] WATER FILTER/PURIFIER OR TREATME
[ ] FOOD/SNACKS (BARS, CHEWS, TRA
      MIX, DRINK MIX)

EMERGENCY ITEMS

[ ] FIRST-AID KIT OR SUPPLIES
[ ] WHISTLE
[ ] LIGHTER/MATCHES (WATERPROOF)
[ ] FIRE STARTER (FOR SURVIVAL FIRE)
[ ] EMERGENCY SHELTER
[ ] TWO ITINERARIES:
      1 LEFT WITH FRIEND + 1 UNDER CAR SE.

EXTRAS

[ ] CAMERA (EXTRA MEMORY CARDS)
[ ] INTERPRETIVE FIELD GUIDE(S)
[ ] JOURNAL/SKETCHBOOK & PEN/PENC
[ ] COMPACT BINOCULARS
[ ] TWO-WAY RADIOS

PERSONAL ITEMS

[ ] PERMITS (IF NEEDED)
[ ] CREDIT CARD AND/OR CASH ID
[ ] CAR KEYS
[ ] CELL PHONE

PRE-HIKE BASIC CHECKLIST

CLOTHING/FOOTWEAR

[ ] MOISTURE-WICKING
     UNDERWEAR
[ ] MOISTURE-WICKING
     SHIRT/PANTS/SHORTS
[ ] BOOTS/SHOES FOR TERRAIN
[ ] SOCKS (SYNTHETIC OR WOOL)
[ ] EXTRA CLOTHING
[ ] LONG-SLEEVE SHIRTS
     (FOR SUN AND BUGS)

*ADDITIONAL ITEMS FOR RAINY
AND/OR COLD WEATHER:*

[ ] RAINWEAR (JACKET & PANTS)
[ ] LONG UNDERWEAR
[ ] WARM INSULATED JACKET/VEST
[ ] GLOVES
[ ] WARM HAT
[ ] BANDANA OR BUF
[ ] SANDALS (FOR STREAMS AND/OR
     CAMP SHOES)

HEALTH & HYGIENE

[ ] HAND SANITIZER
[ ] MENSTRUAL PRODUCTS
[ ] PRESCRIPTION MEDICATIONS
[ ] PRESCRIPTION GLASSES
[ ] INSECT REPELLENT
[ ] BLISTER TREATMENT SUPPLIES
[ ] SANITATION TROWEL
[ ] TOILET PAPER/WIPES AND
     SEALABLE BAG (TO PACK IT OUT)

SUN PROTECTION:
[ ] SUNGLASSES (+ RETAINER LEASH)
[ ] SUNSCREEN
[ ] SPF-RATED LIP BALM
[ ] SUN HAT

TOOLS & REPAIR

[ ] KNIFE OR MULTI-TOOL
[ ] DUCT TAPE

NAVIGATION

[ ] MAP (IN WATERPROOF SLEEVE)
[ ] COMPASS
[ ] ROUTE MAP/GUIDE
[ ] ALTIMETER WATCH
[ ] GPS
[ ] SATELLITE MESSENGER/LOCATOR BEACON

BACKPACKING

[ ] BACKPACK
[ ] HEADLAMP/FLASHLIGHT
[ ] TREKKING POLES
[ ] PACKABLE LANTERN
[ ] BEAR SPRAY

FOOD & WATER

[ ] WATER BOTTLES AND/OR RESERVOIR
[ ] WATER FILTER/PURIFIER OR TREATMENT
[ ] FOOD/SNACKS (BARS, CHEWS, TRAIL
     MIX, DRINK MIX)

EMERGENCY ITEMS

[ ] FIRST-AID KIT OR SUPPLIES
[ ] WHISTLE
[ ] LIGHTER/MATCHES (WATERPROOF)
[ ] FIRE STARTER (FOR SURVIVAL FIRE)
[ ] EMERGENCY SHELTER
[ ] TWO ITINERARIES:
     1 LEFT WITH FRIEND + 1 UNDER CAR SEAT

EXTRAS

[ ] CAMERA (EXTRA MEMORY CARDS)
[ ] INTERPRETIVE FIELD GUIDE(S)
[ ] JOURNAL/SKETCHBOOK & PEN/PENCIL
[ ] COMPACT BINOCULARS
[ ] TWO-WAY RADIOS

PERSONAL ITEMS

[ ] PERMITS (IF NEEDED)
[ ] CREDIT CARD AND/OR CASH ID
[ ] CAR KEYS
[ ] CELL PHONE

PRE-HIKE BASIC CHECKLIST

CLOTHING/FOOTWEAR

[ ] MOISTURE-WICKING
UNDERWEAR
[ ] MOISTURE-WICKING
SHIRT/PANTS/SHORTS
[ ] BOOTS/SHOES FOR TERRAIN
[ ] SOCKS (SYNTHETIC OR WOOL)
[ ] EXTRA CLOTHING
[ ] LONG-SLEEVE SHIRTS
(FOR SUN AND BUGS)

*ADDITIONAL ITEMS FOR RAINY
AND/OR COLD WEATHER:*
[ ] RAINWEAR (JACKET & PANTS)
[ ] LONG UNDERWEAR
[ ] WARM INSULATED JACKET/VEST
[ ] GLOVES
[ ] WARM HAT
[ ] BANDANA OR BUF
[ ] SANDALS (FOR STREAMS AND/OR
CAMP SHOES)

HEALTH & HYGIENE

[ ] HAND SANITIZER
[ ] MENSTRUAL PRODUCTS
[ ] PRESCRIPTION MEDICATIONS
[ ] PRESCRIPTION GLASSES
[ ] INSECT REPELLENT
[ ] BLISTER TREATMENT SUPPLIES
[ ] SANITATION TROWEL
[ ] TOILET PAPER/WIPES AND
SEALABLE BAG (TO PACK IT OUT)

SUN PROTECTION:
[ ] SUNGLASSES (+ RETAINER LEASH)
[ ] SUNSCREEN
[ ] SPF-RATED LIP BALM
[ ] SUN HAT

TOOLS & REPAIR

[ ] KNIFE OR MULTI-TOOL
[ ] DUCT TAPE

NAVIGATION

[ ] MAP (IN WATERPROOF SLEEVE)
[ ] COMPASS
[ ] ROUTE MAP/GUIDE
[ ] ALTIMETER WATCH
[ ] GPS
[ ] SATELLITE MSSGR/LOCATOR BEACON

BACKPACKING

[ ] BACKPACK
[ ] HEADLAMP/FLASHLIGHT
[ ] TREKKING POLES
[ ] PACKABLE LANTERN
[ ] BEAR SPRAY

FOOD & WATER

[ ] WATER BOTTLES AND/OR RESERVOIR
[ ] WATER FILTER/PURIFIER OR TREATMEN
[ ] FOOD/SNACKS (BARS, CHEWS, TRAIL
MIX, DRINK MIX)

EMERGENCY ITEMS

[ ] FIRST-AID KIT OR SUPPLIES
[ ] WHISTLE
[ ] LIGHTER/MATCHES (WATERPROOF)
[ ] FIRE STARTER (FOR SURVIVAL FIRE)
[ ] EMERGENCY SHELTER
[ ] TWO ITINERARIES:
1 LEFT WITH FRIEND + 1 UNDER CAR SEAT

EXTRAS

[ ] CAMERA (EXTRA MEMORY CARDS)
[ ] INTERPRETIVE FIELD GUIDE(S)
[ ] JOURNAL/SKETCHBOOK & PEN/PENCI
[ ] COMPACT BINOCULARS
[ ] TWO-WAY RADIOS

PERSONAL ITEMS

[ ] PERMITS (IF NEEDED)
[ ] CREDIT CARD AND/OR CASH ID
[ ] CAR KEYS
[ ] CELL PHONE

PRE-HIKE BASIC CHECKLIST

CLOTHING/FOOTWEAR

[ ] MOISTURE-WICKING
    UNDERWEAR
[ ] MOISTURE-WICKING
    SHIRT/PANTS/SHORTS
[ ] BOOTS/SHOES FOR TERRAIN
[ ] SOCKS (SYNTHETIC OR WOOL)
[ ] EXTRA CLOTHING
[ ] LONG-SLEEVE SHIRTS
    (FOR SUN AND BUGS)

*ADDITIONAL ITEMS FOR RAINY
AND/OR COLD WEATHER:*

[ ] RAINWEAR (JACKET & PANTS)
[ ] LONG UNDERWEAR
[ ] WARM INSULATED JACKET/VEST
[ ] GLOVES
[ ] WARM HAT
[ ] BANDANA OR BUF
[ ] SANDALS (FOR STREAMS AND/OR
    CAMP SHOES)

HEALTH & HYGIENE

[ ] HAND SANITIZER
[ ] MENSTRUAL PRODUCTS
[ ] PRESCRIPTION MEDICATIONS
[ ] PRESCRIPTION GLASSES
[ ] INSECT REPELLENT
[ ] BLISTER TREATMENT SUPPLIES
[ ] SANITATION TROWEL
[ ] TOILET PAPER/WIPES AND
    SEALABLE BAG (TO PACK IT OUT)

SUN PROTECTION:

[ ] SUNGLASSES (+ RETAINER LEASH)
[ ] SUNSCREEN
[ ] SPF-RATED LIP BALM
[ ] SUN HAT

TOOLS & REPAIR

[ ] KNIFE OR MULTI-TOOL
[ ] DUCT TAPE

NAVIGATION

[ ] MAP (IN WATERPROOF SLEEVE)
[ ] COMPASS
[ ] ROUTE MAP/GUIDE
[ ] ALTIMETER WATCH
[ ] GPS
[ ] SATELLITE MESSENGER/LOCATOR BEACON

BACKPACKING

[ ] BACKPACK
[ ] HEADLAMP/FLASHLIGHT
[ ] TREKKING POLES
[ ] PACKABLE LANTERN
[ ] BEAR SPRAY

FOOD & WATER

[ ] WATER BOTTLES AND/OR RESERVOIR
[ ] WATER FILTER/PURIFIER OR TREATMENT
[ ] FOOD/SNACKS (BARS, CHEWS, TRAIL
    MIX, DRINK MIX)

EMERGENCY ITEMS

[ ] FIRST-AID KIT OR SUPPLIES
[ ] WHISTLE
[ ] LIGHTER/MATCHES (WATERPROOF)
[ ] FIRE STARTER (FOR SURVIVAL FIRE)
[ ] EMERGENCY SHELTER
[ ] TWO ITINERARIES:
    1 LEFT WITH FRIEND + 1 UNDER CAR SEAT

EXTRAS

[ ] CAMERA (EXTRA MEMORY CARDS)
[ ] INTERPRETIVE FIELD GUIDE(S)
[ ] JOURNAL/SKETCHBOOK & PEN/PENCIL
[ ] COMPACT BINOCULARS
[ ] TWO-WAY RADIOS

PERSONAL ITEMS

[ ] PERMITS (IF NEEDED)
[ ] CREDIT CARD AND/OR CASH ID
[ ] CAR KEYS
[ ] CELL PHONE

PRE-HIKE BASIC CHECKLIST

CLOTHING/FOOTWEAR

[ ] MOISTURE-WICKING
    UNDERWEAR
[ ] MOISTURE-WICKING
    SHIRT/PANTS/SHORTS
[ ] BOOTS/SHOES FOR TERRAIN
[ ] SOCKS (SYNTHETIC OR WOOL)
[ ] EXTRA CLOTHING
[ ] LONG-SLEEVE SHIRTS
    (FOR SUN AND BUGS)

*ADDITIONAL ITEMS FOR RAINY
AND/OR COLD WEATHER:*
[ ] RAINWEAR (JACKET & PANTS)
[ ] LONG UNDERWEAR
[ ] WARM INSULATED JACKET/VEST
[ ] GLOVES
[ ] WARM HAT
[ ] BANDANA OR BUF
[ ] SANDALS (FOR STREAMS AND/OR
    CAMP SHOES)

HEALTH & HYGIENE

[ ] HAND SANITIZER
[ ] MENSTRUAL PRODUCTS
[ ] PRESCRIPTION MEDICATIONS
[ ] PRESCRIPTION GLASSES
[ ] INSECT REPELLENT
[ ] BLISTER TREATMENT SUPPLIES
[ ] SANITATION TROWEL
[ ] TOILET PAPER/WIPES AND
    SEALABLE BAG (TO PACK IT OUT)

SUN PROTECTION:
[ ] SUNGLASSES (+ RETAINER LEASH)
[ ] SUNSCREEN
[ ] SPF-RATED LIP BALM
[ ] SUN HAT

TOOLS & REPAIR

[ ] KNIFE OR MULTI-TOOL
[ ] DUCT TAPE

NAVIGATION

[ ] MAP (IN WATERPROOF SLEEVE)
[ ] COMPASS
[ ] ROUTE MAP/GUIDE
[ ] ALTIMETER WATCH
[ ] GPS
[ ] SATELLITE MSSGR/LOCATOR BEACON

BACKPACKING

[ ] BACKPACK
[ ] HEADLAMP/FLASHLIGHT
[ ] TREKKING POLES
[ ] PACKABLE LANTERN
[ ] BEAR SPRAY

FOOD & WATER

[ ] WATER BOTTLES AND/OR RESERVOIR
[ ] WATER FILTER/PURIFIER OR TREATMEN
[ ] FOOD/SNACKS (BARS, CHEWS, TRAIL
    MIX, DRINK MIX)

EMERGENCY ITEMS

[ ] FIRST-AID KIT OR SUPPLIES
[ ] WHISTLE
[ ] LIGHTER/MATCHES (WATERPROOF)
[ ] FIRE STARTER (FOR SURVIVAL FIRE)
[ ] EMERGENCY SHELTER
[ ] TWO ITINERARIES:
    1 LEFT WITH FRIEND + 1 UNDER CAR SEAT

EXTRAS

[ ] CAMERA (EXTRA MEMORY CARDS)
[ ] INTERPRETIVE FIELD GUIDE(S)
[ ] JOURNAL/SKETCHBOOK & PEN/PENCIL
[ ] COMPACT BINOCULARS
[ ] TWO-WAY RADIOS

PERSONAL ITEMS

[ ] PERMITS (IF NEEDED)
[ ] CREDIT CARD AND/OR CASH ID
[ ] CAR KEYS
[ ] CELL PHONE

RE-HIKE BASIC CHECKLIST

CLOTHING/FOOTWEAR

- MOISTURE-WICKING UNDERWEAR
- MOISTURE-WICKING SHIRT/PANTS/SHORTS
- BOOTS/SHOES FOR TERRAIN
- SOCKS (SYNTHETIC OR WOOL)
- EXTRA CLOTHING
- LONG-SLEEVE SHIRTS (FOR SUN AND BUGS)

ADDITIONAL ITEMS FOR RAINY AND/OR COLD WEATHER:

- RAINWEAR (JACKET & PANTS)
- LONG UNDERWEAR
- WARM INSULATED JACKET/VEST
- GLOVES
- WARM HAT
- BANDANA OR BUF
- SANDALS (FOR STREAMS AND/OR CAMP SHOES)

HEALTH & HYGIENE

- HAND SANITIZER
- MENSTRUAL PRODUCTS
- PRESCRIPTION MEDICATIONS
- PRESCRIPTION GLASSES
- INSECT REPELLENT
- BLISTER TREATMENT SUPPLIES
- SANITATION TROWEL
- TOILET PAPER/WIPES AND SEALABLE BAG (TO PACK IT OUT)

SUN PROTECTION:

- SUNGLASSES (+ RETAINER LEASH)
- SUNSCREEN
- SPF-RATED LIP BALM
- SUN HAT

TOOLS & REPAIR

- KNIFE OR MULTI-TOOL
- DUCT TAPE

NAVIGATION

- [ ] MAP (IN WATERPROOF SLEEVE)
- [ ] COMPASS
- [ ] ROUTE MAP/GUIDE
- [ ] ALTIMETER WATCH
- [ ] GPS
- [ ] SATELLITE MESSENGER/LOCATOR BEACON

BACKPACKING

- [ ] BACKPACK
- [ ] HEADLAMP/FLASHLIGHT
- [ ] TREKKING POLES
- [ ] PACKABLE LANTERN
- [ ] BEAR SPRAY

FOOD & WATER

- [ ] WATER BOTTLES AND/OR RESERVOIR
- [ ] WATER FILTER/PURIFIER OR TREATMENT
- [ ] FOOD/SNACKS (BARS, CHEWS, TRAIL MIX, DRINK MIX)

EMERGENCY ITEMS

- [ ] FIRST-AID KIT OR SUPPLIES
- [ ] WHISTLE
- [ ] LIGHTER/MATCHES (WATERPROOF)
- [ ] FIRE STARTER (FOR SURVIVAL FIRE)
- [ ] EMERGENCY SHELTER
- [ ] TWO ITINERARIES: 1 LEFT WITH FRIEND + 1 UNDER CAR SEAT

EXTRAS

- [ ] CAMERA (EXTRA MEMORY CARDS)
- [ ] INTERPRETIVE FIELD GUIDE(S)
- [ ] JOURNAL/SKETCHBOOK & PEN/PENCIL
- [ ] COMPACT BINOCULARS
- [ ] TWO-WAY RADIOS

PERSONAL ITEMS

- [ ] PERMITS (IF NEEDED)
- [ ] CREDIT CARD AND/OR CASH ID
- [ ] CAR KEYS
- [ ] CELL PHONE

PRE-HIKE BASIC CHECKLIST

CLOTHING/FOOTWEAR

[ ] MOISTURE-WICKING
    UNDERWEAR
[ ] MOISTURE-WICKING
    SHIRT/PANTS/SHORTS
[ ] BOOTS/SHOES FOR TERRAIN
[ ] SOCKS (SYNTHETIC OR WOOL)
[ ] EXTRA CLOTHING
[ ] LONG-SLEEVE SHIRTS
    (FOR SUN AND BUGS)

*ADDITIONAL ITEMS FOR RAINY
AND/OR COLD WEATHER:*
[ ] RAINWEAR (JACKET & PANTS)
[ ] LONG UNDERWEAR
[ ] WARM INSULATED JACKET/VEST
[ ] GLOVES
[ ] WARM HAT
[ ] BANDANA OR BUF
[ ] SANDALS (FOR STREAMS AND/OR
    CAMP SHOES)

HEALTH & HYGIENE

[ ] HAND SANITIZER
[ ] MENSTRUAL PRODUCTS
[ ] PRESCRIPTION MEDICATIONS
[ ] PRESCRIPTION GLASSES
[ ] INSECT REPELLENT
[ ] BLISTER TREATMENT SUPPLIES
[ ] SANITATION TROWEL
[ ] TOILET PAPER/WIPES AND
    SEALABLE BAG (TO PACK IT OUT)

SUN PROTECTION:
[ ] SUNGLASSES (+ RETAINER LEASH)
[ ] SUNSCREEN
[ ] SPF-RATED LIP BALM
[ ] SUN HAT

TOOLS & REPAIR

[ ] KNIFE OR MULTI-TOOL
[ ] DUCT TAPE

NAVIGATION

[ ] MAP (IN WATERPROOF SLEEVE)
[ ] COMPASS
[ ] ROUTE MAP/GUIDE
[ ] ALTIMETER WATCH
[ ] GPS
[ ] SATELLITE MSSGR/LOCATOR BEACO

BACKPACKING

[ ] BACKPACK
[ ] HEADLAMP/FLASHLIGHT
[ ] TREKKING POLES
[ ] PACKABLE LANTERN
[ ] BEAR SPRAY

FOOD & WATER

[ ] WATER BOTTLES AND/OR RESERVOIR
[ ] WATER FILTER/PURIFIER OR TREATME
[ ] FOOD/SNACKS (BARS, CHEWS, TRA
    MIX, DRINK MIX)

EMERGENCY ITEMS

[ ] FIRST-AID KIT OR SUPPLIES
[ ] WHISTLE
[ ] LIGHTER/MATCHES (WATERPROOF)
[ ] FIRE STARTER (FOR SURVIVAL FIRE)
[ ] EMERGENCY SHELTER
[ ] TWO ITINERARIES:
    1 LEFT WITH FRIEND + 1 UNDER CAR SE.

EXTRAS

[ ] CAMERA (EXTRA MEMORY CARDS)
[ ] INTERPRETIVE FIELD GUIDE(S)
[ ] JOURNAL/SKETCHBOOK & PEN/PENC
[ ] COMPACT BINOCULARS
[ ] TWO-WAY RADIOS

PERSONAL ITEMS

[ ] PERMITS (IF NEEDED)
[ ] CREDIT CARD AND/OR CASH ID
[ ] CAR KEYS
[ ] CELL PHONE

PRE-HIKE BASIC CHECKLIST

CLOTHING/FOOTWEAR

[ ] MOISTURE-WICKING
    UNDERWEAR
[ ] MOISTURE-WICKING
    SHIRT/PANTS/SHORTS
[ ] BOOTS/SHOES FOR TERRAIN
[ ] SOCKS (SYNTHETIC OR WOOL)
[ ] EXTRA CLOTHING
[ ] LONG-SLEEVE SHIRTS
    (FOR SUN AND BUGS)

*ADDITIONAL ITEMS FOR RAINY
AND/OR COLD WEATHER:*

[ ] RAINWEAR (JACKET & PANTS)
[ ] LONG UNDERWEAR
[ ] WARM INSULATED JACKET/VEST
[ ] GLOVES
[ ] WARM HAT
[ ] BANDANA OR BUF
[ ] SANDALS (FOR STREAMS AND/OR
    CAMP SHOES)

HEALTH & HYGIENE

[ ] HAND SANITIZER
[ ] MENSTRUAL PRODUCTS
[ ] PRESCRIPTION MEDICATIONS
[ ] PRESCRIPTION GLASSES
[ ] INSECT REPELLENT
[ ] BLISTER TREATMENT SUPPLIES
[ ] SANITATION TROWEL
[ ] TOILET PAPER/WIPES AND
    SEALABLE BAG (TO PACK IT OUT)

SUN PROTECTION:
[ ] SUNGLASSES (+ RETAINER LEASH)
[ ] SUNSCREEN
[ ] SPF-RATED LIP BALM
[ ] SUN HAT

TOOLS & REPAIR

[ ] KNIFE OR MULTI-TOOL
[ ] DUCT TAPE

NAVIGATION

[ ] MAP (IN WATERPROOF SLEEVE)
[ ] COMPASS
[ ] ROUTE MAP/GUIDE
[ ] ALTIMETER WATCH
[ ] GPS
[ ] SATELLITE MESSENGER/LOCATOR BEACON

BACKPACKING

[ ] BACKPACK
[ ] HEADLAMP/FLASHLIGHT
[ ] TREKKING POLES
[ ] PACKABLE LANTERN
[ ] BEAR SPRAY

FOOD & WATER

[ ] WATER BOTTLES AND/OR RESERVOIR
[ ] WATER FILTER/PURIFIER OR TREATMENT
[ ] FOOD/SNACKS (BARS, CHEWS, TRAIL
    MIX, DRINK MIX)

EMERGENCY ITEMS

[ ] FIRST-AID KIT OR SUPPLIES
[ ] WHISTLE
[ ] LIGHTER/MATCHES (WATERPROOF)
[ ] FIRE STARTER (FOR SURVIVAL FIRE)
[ ] EMERGENCY SHELTER
[ ] TWO ITINERARIES:
    1 LEFT WITH FRIEND + 1 UNDER CAR SEAT

EXTRAS

[ ] CAMERA (EXTRA MEMORY CARDS)
[ ] INTERPRETIVE FIELD GUIDE(S)
[ ] JOURNAL/SKETCHBOOK & PEN/PENCIL
[ ] COMPACT BINOCULARS
[ ] TWO-WAY RADIOS

PERSONAL ITEMS

[ ] PERMITS (IF NEEDED)
[ ] CREDIT CARD AND/OR CASH ID
[ ] CAR KEYS
[ ] CELL PHONE

BASICS
[ ] 1ST VISIT [ ] 2ND VISIT [ ] 3RD VISIT

DATE: /   /   LOCATION:

TRAIL:

START TIME: :   TEMP RANGE: WEATHER:
END TIME: :
DURATION: ☀ 🌤 ⛅ 🌧 🌬 🌨

COMPANIONS:

FEES: PARKING/SHUTTLES:

BRIEF RECAP OF THE EXPERIENCE:

HIKE SPECIFICS [ ] COMPLETED   [ ] NOT COMPLETED

TRAIL TYPE: [ ] LOOP   [ ] OUT & BACK   [ ] POINT TO POINT

DIFFICULTY: ☆☆☆☆☆ RATING: ☆☆☆☆☆

PRIMARY TERRAIN: [ ] DIRT [ ] ROCK [ ] PAVED [ ] OTHER:

ELEVATION: GAIN/LOSS:_____ START:_____ END:_____

SUITABILITY: [ ] DOG-FRIENDLY [ ] KID-FRIENDLY [ ] STROLLER-FRIENDLY
             [ ] FULLY PAVED [ ] PARTIALLY PAVED [ ] WHEELCHAIR-FRIENDLY

TRAIL LENGTH:_____ COMPLETED: [ ] ALL [ ] OTHER: _____
TRAIL TRAFFIC: [ ] LIGHT [ ] MODERATE [ ] HEAVY
TRAIL ACTIVITIES: [ ] WALKING [ ] ROCK CLIMBING [ ] TRAIL RUNNING
                  [ ] MOUNTAIN BIKING [ ] BIRD WATCHING [ ] CAMPING
                  [ ] HORSEBACK RIDING [ ] OTHER: _____

SCENERY: [ ] NATURE VIEWS [ ] CITY VIEWS [ ] LAKE/RIVER [ ] WATERFALL
         [ ] CLIFFS [ ] FOREST [ ] HISTORIC SITE [ ] HOT SPRINGS
         [ ] WILD FLOWERS [ ] WILDLIFE [ ] OTHER: _____

EXPOSURE: [ ] NONE [ ] MINIMAL [ ] SOME [ ] EXTENSIVE

COVER/SHADE: [ ] FULL SUN [ ] PARTIAL SHADE [ ] MOSTLY SHADE [ ] FULL SHADE

WATER CROSSING: [ ] NONE [ ] ROCK HOP [ ] FOOTBRIDGE [ ] WET CROSSING

NUTRITION:

WATER: | **SNACKS:** | **MEALS:**

MAIN GEAR BROUGHT:

GEAR MISSED:

NOTES FOR NEXT TRIP:

BASICS

[ ] 1ST VISIT [ ] 2ND VISIT [ ] 3RD VISIT

DATE: / /   LOCATION:

TRAIL:

START TIME: :   TEMP RANGE: WEATHER:
END TIME: :
DURATION: ☀ 🌤 🌦 🌧 💨 ❄

COMPANIONS:

FEES: PARKING/SHUTTLES:

BRIEF RECAP OF THE EXPERIENCE:

HIKE SPECIFICS [ ] COMPLETED   [ ] NOT COMPLETED

TRAIL TYPE: [ ] LOOP   [ ] OUT & BACK [ ] POINT TO POINT

DIFFICULTY: ☆☆☆☆☆ RATING: ☆☆☆☆☆

PRIMARY TERRAIN: [ ] DIRT [ ] ROCK [ ] PAVED [ ] OTHER:

ELEVATION: GAIN/LOSS:_____ START:_____ END:_____

SUITABILITY: [ ] DOG-FRIENDLY [ ] KID-FRIENDLY [ ] STROLLER-FRIENDLY
            [ ] FULLY PAVED [ ] PARTIALLY PAVED [ ] WHEELCHAIR-FRIENDLY

TRAIL LENGTH:_____ COMPLETED: [ ] ALL [ ] OTHER: _____
TRAIL TRAFFIC: [ ] LIGHT [ ] MODERATE [ ] HEAVY
TRAIL ACTIVITIES: [ ] WALKING [ ] ROCK CLIMBING [ ] TRAIL RUNNING
                 [ ] MOUNTAIN BIKING [ ] BIRD WATCHING [ ] CAMPING
                 [ ] HORSEBACK RIDING [ ] OTHER: _____

SCENERY: [ ] NATURE VIEWS [ ] CITY VIEWS [ ] LAKE/RIVER [ ] WATERFALL
        [ ] CLIFFS [ ] FOREST [ ] HISTORIC SITE [ ] HOT SPRINGS
        [ ] WILD FLOWERS [ ] WILDLIFE [ ] OTHER: _____

EXPOSURE: [ ] NONE [ ] MINIMAL [ ] SOME [ ] EXTENSIVE
COVER/SHADE: [ ] FULL SUN [ ] PARTIAL SHADE [ ] MOSTLY SHADE [ ] FULL SHADE
WATER CROSSING: [ ] NONE [ ] ROCK HOP [ ] FOOTBRIDGE [ ] WET CROSSING

NUTRITION:

WATER: | **SNACKS:** | **MEALS:**

MAIN GEAR BROUGHT:

GEAR MISSED:

NOTES FOR NEXT TRIP:

BASICS

[ ] 1ST VISIT [ ] 2ND VISIT [ ] 3RD VISIT

DATE: /   /   LOCATION:

TRAIL:

START TIME: :   TEMP RANGE: WEATHER:
END TIME: :
DURATION: ☀ ⛅ ☁ 🌧 🌬 ❄

COMPANIONS:

FEES: PARKING/SHUTTLES:

BRIEF RECAP OF THE EXPERIENCE:

HIKE SPECIFICS [ ] COMPLETED   [ ] NOT COMPLETED

TRAIL TYPE: [ ] LOOP   [ ] OUT & BACK   [ ] POINT TO POINT

DIFFICULTY: ☆☆☆☆☆ RATING: ☆☆☆☆☆

PRIMARY TERRAIN: [ ] DIRT [ ] ROCK [ ] PAVED [ ] OTHER:

ELEVATION: GAIN/LOSS:_____ START:_____ END:_____

SUITABILITY: [ ] DOG-FRIENDLY [ ] KID-FRIENDLY [ ] STROLLER-FRIENDLY
             [ ] FULLY PAVED [ ] PARTIALLY PAVED [ ] WHEELCHAIR-FRIENDLY

TRAIL LENGTH:_____ COMPLETED: [ ] ALL [ ] OTHER: _____
TRAIL TRAFFIC: [ ] LIGHT [ ] MODERATE [ ] HEAVY
TRAIL ACTIVITIES: [ ] WALKING [ ] ROCK CLIMBING [ ] TRAIL RUNNING
                  [ ] MOUNTAIN BIKING [ ] BIRD WATCHING [ ] CAMPING
                  [ ] HORSEBACK RIDING [ ] OTHER: _____

SCENERY: [ ] NATURE VIEWS [ ] CITY VIEWS [ ] LAKE/RIVER [ ] WATERFALL
         [ ] CLIFFS [ ] FOREST [ ] HISTORIC SITE [ ] HOT SPRINGS
         [ ] WILD FLOWERS [ ] WILDLIFE [ ] OTHER: _____

EXPOSURE: [ ] NONE [ ] MINIMAL [ ] SOME [ ] EXTENSIVE
COVER/SHADE: [ ] FULL SUN [ ] PARTIAL SHADE [ ] MOSTLY SHADE [ ] FULL SHAD
WATER CROSSING: [ ] NONE [ ] ROCK HOP [ ] FOOTBRIDGE [ ] WET CROSSING

NUTRITION:

WATER: | **SNACKS:** | **MEALS:**

MAIN GEAR BROUGHT:

GEAR MISSED:

NOTES FOR NEXT TRIP:

BASICS

[ ] 1ST VISIT [ ] 2ND VISIT [ ] 3RD VISIT

DATE: /   /   LOCATION:

TRAIL:

START TIME: :   TEMP RANGE: WEATHER:
END TIME: :
DURATION: ☀ ⛅ ☁ 🌧 💨 ❄

COMPANIONS:

FEES: PARKING/SHUTTLES:

BRIEF RECAP OF THE EXPERIENCE:

HIKE SPECIFICS [ ] COMPLETED   [ ] NOT COMPLETED

TRAIL TYPE: [ ] LOOP   [ ] OUT & BACK   [ ] POINT TO POINT

DIFFICULTY: ☆☆☆☆☆ RATING: ☆☆☆☆☆

PRIMARY TERRAIN: [ ] DIRT [ ] ROCK [ ] PAVED [ ] OTHER:

ELEVATION: GAIN/LOSS:_____ START:_____ END:_____

SUITABILITY: [ ] DOG-FRIENDLY [ ] KID-FRIENDLY [ ] STROLLER-FRIENDLY
            [ ] FULLY PAVED [ ] PARTIALLY PAVED [ ] WHEELCHAIR-FRIENDLY

TRAIL LENGTH:_____ COMPLETED: [ ] ALL [ ] OTHER: _____
TRAIL TRAFFIC: [ ] LIGHT [ ] MODERATE [ ] HEAVY
TRAIL ACTIVITIES: [ ] WALKING [ ] ROCK CLIMBING [ ] TRAIL RUNNING
                [ ] MOUNTAIN BIKING [ ] BIRD WATCHING [ ] CAMPING
                [ ] HORSEBACK RIDING [ ] OTHER: _____

SCENERY: [ ] NATURE VIEWS [ ] CITY VIEWS [ ] LAKE/RIVER [ ] WATERFALL
        [ ] CLIFFS [ ] FOREST [ ] HISTORIC SITE [ ] HOT SPRINGS
        [ ] WILD FLOWERS [ ] WILDLIFE [ ] OTHER: _____

EXPOSURE: [ ] NONE [ ] MINIMAL [ ] SOME [ ] EXTENSIVE

COVER/SHADE: [ ] FULL SUN [ ] PARTIAL SHADE [ ] MOSTLY SHADE [ ] FULL SHADE

WATER CROSSING: [ ] NONE [ ] ROCK HOP [ ] FOOTBRIDGE [ ] WET CROSSING

NUTRITION:

WATER: | **SNACKS:** | **MEALS:**

MAIN GEAR BROUGHT:

GEAR MISSED:

NOTES FOR NEXT TRIP:

BASICS

[ ] 1ST VISIT [ ] 2ND VISIT [ ] 3RD VISIT

DATE: /   /   LOCATION:

TRAIL:

START TIME: :	TEMP RANGE:	WEATHER:
END TIME: :		☀ 🌤 ⛅ 🌧 💨 ❄
DURATION:		

COMPANIONS:

FEES: PARKING/SHUTTLES:

BRIEF RECAP OF THE EXPERIENCE:

HIKE SPECIFICS [ ] COMPLETED   [ ] NOT COMPLETED

TRAIL TYPE: [ ] LOOP   [ ] OUT & BACK   [ ] POINT TO POINT

DIFFICULTY: ☆☆☆☆☆ RATING: ☆☆☆☆☆

PRIMARY TERRAIN: [ ] DIRT [ ] ROCK [ ] PAVED [ ] OTHER:

ELEVATION: GAIN/LOSS:_____ START:_____ END:_____

SUITABILITY: [ ] DOG-FRIENDLY [ ] KID-FRIENDLY [ ] STROLLER-FRIENDLY
             [ ] FULLY PAVED [ ] PARTIALLY PAVED [ ] WHEELCHAIR-FRIENDLY

TRAIL LENGTH:_____ COMPLETED: [ ] ALL [ ] OTHER: _____
TRAIL TRAFFIC: [ ] LIGHT [ ] MODERATE [ ] HEAVY
TRAIL ACTIVITIES: [ ] WALKING [ ] ROCK CLIMBING [ ] TRAIL RUNNING
                  [ ] MOUNTAIN BIKING [ ] BIRD WATCHING [ ] CAMPING
                  [ ] HORSEBACK RIDING [ ] OTHER: _____

SCENERY: [ ] NATURE VIEWS [ ] CITY VIEWS [ ] LAKE/RIVER [ ] WATERFALL
         [ ] CLIFFS [ ] FOREST [ ] HISTORIC SITE [ ] HOT SPRINGS
         [ ] WILD FLOWERS [ ] WILDLIFE [ ] OTHER: _____

EXPOSURE: [ ] NONE [ ] MINIMAL [ ] SOME [ ] EXTENSIVE

COVER/SHADE: [ ] FULL SUN [ ] PARTIAL SHADE [ ] MOSTLY SHADE [ ] FULL SHADE

WATER CROSSING: [ ] NONE [ ] ROCK HOP [ ] FOOTBRIDGE [ ] WET CROSSING

NUTRITION:

WATER: | **SNACKS:** | **MEALS:**

MAIN GEAR BROUGHT:

GEAR MISSED:

NOTES FOR NEXT TRIP:

BASICS

[ ] 1ST VISIT [ ] 2ND VISIT [ ] 3RD VISIT

DATE: / /   LOCATION:

TRAIL:

START TIME: : | TEMP RANGE: | WEATHER:
END TIME: : | | ☀ ⛅ ☁ 🌧 🌬 ❄
DURATION: | |

COMPANIONS:

FEES: PARKING/SHUTTLES:

BRIEF RECAP OF THE EXPERIENCE:

HIKE SPECIFICS [ ] COMPLETED   [ ] NOT COMPLETED

TRAIL TYPE: [ ] LOOP   [ ] OUT & BACK   [ ] POINT TO POINT

DIFFICULTY: ☆☆☆☆☆ RATING: ☆☆☆☆☆

PRIMARY TERRAIN: [ ] DIRT [ ] ROCK [ ] PAVED [ ] OTHER:

ELEVATION: GAIN/LOSS:_____ START:_____ END:_____

SUITABILITY: [ ] DOG-FRIENDLY [ ] KID-FRIENDLY [ ] STROLLER-FRIENDLY
             [ ] FULLY PAVED [ ] PARTIALLY PAVED [ ] WHEELCHAIR-FRIENDLY

TRAIL LENGTH:_____ COMPLETED: [ ] ALL [ ] OTHER: _____
TRAIL TRAFFIC: [ ] LIGHT [ ] MODERATE [ ] HEAVY
TRAIL ACTIVITIES: [ ] WALKING [ ] ROCK CLIMBING [ ] TRAIL RUNNING
                 [ ] MOUNTAIN BIKING [ ] BIRD WATCHING [ ] CAMPING
                 [ ] HORSEBACK RIDING [ ] OTHER: _____

SCENERY: [ ] NATURE VIEWS [ ] CITY VIEWS [ ] LAKE/RIVER [ ] WATERFALL
         [ ] CLIFFS [ ] FOREST [ ] HISTORIC SITE [ ] HOT SPRINGS
         [ ] WILD FLOWERS [ ] WILDLIFE [ ] OTHER: _____

EXPOSURE: [ ] NONE [ ] MINIMAL [ ] SOME [ ] EXTENSIVE

COVER/SHADE: [ ] FULL SUN [ ] PARTIAL SHADE [ ] MOSTLY SHADE [ ] FULL SHAD

WATER CROSSING: [ ] NONE [ ] ROCK HOP [ ] FOOTBRIDGE [ ] WET CROSSING

NUTRITION:

WATER: | **SNACKS:** | **MEALS:**

MAIN GEAR BROUGHT:

GEAR MISSED:

NOTES FOR NEXT TRIP:

BASICS

[ ] 1ST VISIT [ ] 2ND VISIT [ ] 3RD VISIT

DATE: / / LOCATION:

TRAIL:

START TIME: :   TEMP RANGE: WEATHER:
END TIME: :
DURATION: ☼ ☼ ☁ ☁ 💨 ❄

COMPANIONS:

FEES: PARKING/SHUTTLES:

BRIEF RECAP OF THE EXPERIENCE:

HIKE SPECIFICS [ ] COMPLETED [ ] NOT COMPLETED

TRAIL TYPE: [ ] LOOP [ ] OUT & BACK [ ] POINT TO POINT

DIFFICULTY: ☆☆☆☆☆ RATING: ☆☆☆☆☆

PRIMARY TERRAIN: [ ] DIRT [ ] ROCK [ ] PAVED [ ] OTHER:

ELEVATION: GAIN/LOSS:_____ START:_____ END:_____

SUITABILITY: [ ] DOG-FRIENDLY [ ] KID-FRIENDLY [ ] STROLLER-FRIENDLY
[ ] FULLY PAVED [ ] PARTIALLY PAVED [ ] WHEELCHAIR-FRIENDLY

TRAIL LENGTH:_____ COMPLETED: [ ] ALL [ ] OTHER: _____
TRAIL TRAFFIC: [ ] LIGHT [ ] MODERATE [ ] HEAVY
TRAIL ACTIVITIES: [ ] WALKING [ ] ROCK CLIMBING [ ] TRAIL RUNNING
[ ] MOUNTAIN BIKING [ ] BIRD WATCHING [ ] CAMPING
[ ] HORSEBACK RIDING [ ] OTHER: _____

SCENERY: [ ] NATURE VIEWS [ ] CITY VIEWS [ ] LAKE/RIVER [ ] WATERFALL
[ ] CLIFFS [ ] FOREST [ ] HISTORIC SITE [ ] HOT SPRINGS
[ ] WILD FLOWERS [ ] WILDLIFE [ ] OTHER: _____

EXPOSURE: [ ] NONE [ ] MINIMAL [ ] SOME [ ] EXTENSIVE

COVER/SHADE: [ ] FULL SUN [ ] PARTIAL SHADE [ ] MOSTLY SHADE [ ] FULL SHADE

WATER CROSSING: [ ] NONE [ ] ROCK HOP [ ] FOOTBRIDGE [ ] WET CROSSING

NUTRITION:

WATER: | **SNACKS:** | **MEALS:**

MAIN GEAR BROUGHT:

GEAR MISSED:

NOTES FOR NEXT TRIP:

BASICS

[ ] 1ST VISIT   [ ] 2ND VISIT   [ ] 3RD VISIT

DATE: /   /   LOCATION:

TRAIL:

START TIME: :   TEMP RANGE: WEATHER:
END TIME: :
DURATION: ☀ 🌤 ⛅ 🌧 🌬 ❄

COMPANIONS:

FEES: PARKING/SHUTTLES:

BRIEF RECAP OF THE EXPERIENCE:

HIKE SPECIFICS   [ ] COMPLETED   [ ] NOT COMPLETED

TRAIL TYPE: [ ] LOOP   [ ] OUT & BACK   [ ] POINT TO POINT

DIFFICULTY: ☆☆☆☆☆   RATING: ☆☆☆☆☆

PRIMARY TERRAIN: [ ] DIRT [ ] ROCK [ ] PAVED [ ] OTHER:

ELEVATION: GAIN/LOSS:_____ START:_____ END:_____

SUITABILITY: [ ] DOG-FRIENDLY [ ] KID-FRIENDLY [ ] STROLLER-FRIENDLY
            [ ] FULLY PAVED [ ] PARTIALLY PAVED [ ] WHEELCHAIR-FRIENDLY

TRAIL LENGTH:_____ COMPLETED: [ ] ALL [ ] OTHER: _____
TRAIL TRAFFIC: [ ] LIGHT [ ] MODERATE [ ] HEAVY
TRAIL ACTIVITIES: [ ] WALKING [ ] ROCK CLIMBING [ ] TRAIL RUNNING
                [ ] MOUNTAIN BIKING [ ] BIRD WATCHING [ ] CAMPING
                [ ] HORSEBACK RIDING [ ] OTHER: _____

SCENERY: [ ] NATURE VIEWS [ ] CITY VIEWS [ ] LAKE/RIVER [ ] WATERFALL
        [ ] CLIFFS [ ] FOREST [ ] HISTORIC SITE [ ] HOT SPRINGS
        [ ] WILD FLOWERS [ ] WILDLIFE [ ] OTHER: _____

EXPOSURE: [ ] NONE [ ] MINIMAL [ ] SOME [ ] EXTENSIVE

COVER/SHADE: [ ] FULL SUN [ ] PARTIAL SHADE [ ] MOSTLY SHADE [ ] FULL SHADE

WATER CROSSING: [ ] NONE [ ] ROCK HOP [ ] FOOTBRIDGE [ ] WET CROSSING

NUTRITION:

WATER:	SNACKS:	MEALS:

MAIN GEAR BROUGHT:

GEAR MISSED:

NOTES FOR NEXT TRIP:

BASICS

[ ] 1ST VISIT [ ] 2ND VISIT [ ] 3RD VISIT

DATE: /   /   LOCATION:

TRAIL:

START TIME: :	TEMP RANGE:	WEATHER:
END TIME: :		☀ 🌤 ⛅ ☁ 🌬 ❄
DURATION:		

COMPANIONS:

FEES: PARKING/SHUTTLES:

BRIEF RECAP OF THE EXPERIENCE:

HIKE SPECIFICS [ ] COMPLETED   [ ] NOT COMPLETED

TRAIL TYPE: [ ] LOOP   [ ] OUT & BACK   [ ] POINT TO POINT

DIFFICULTY: ☆☆☆☆☆ RATING: ☆☆☆☆☆

PRIMARY TERRAIN:[ ] DIRT [ ] ROCK [ ] PAVED [ ] OTHER:

ELEVATION: GAIN/LOSS:_____ START:_____ END:_____

SUITABILITY: [ ] DOG-FRIENDLY [ ] KID-FRIENDLY [ ] STROLLER-FRIENDLY
             [ ] FULLY PAVED [ ] PARTIALLY PAVED [ ] WHEELCHAIR-FRIENDLY

TRAIL LENGTH:_____ COMPLETED: [ ] ALL [ ] OTHER: _____
TRAIL TRAFFIC: [ ] LIGHT [ ] MODERATE [ ] HEAVY
TRAIL ACTIVITIES: [ ] WALKING [ ] ROCK CLIMBING [ ] TRAIL RUNNING
                  [ ] MOUNTAIN BIKING [ ] BIRD WATCHING [ ] CAMPING
                  [ ] HORSEBACK RIDING [ ] OTHER: _____

SCENERY: [ ] NATURE VIEWS [ ] CITY VIEWS [ ] LAKE/RIVER [ ] WATERFALL
         [ ] CLIFFS [ ] FOREST [ ] HISTORIC SITE [ ] HOT SPRINGS
         [ ] WILD FLOWERS [ ] WILDLIFE [ ] OTHER: _____

EXPOSURE: [ ] NONE [ ] MINIMAL [ ] SOME [ ] EXTENSIVE
COVER/SHADE: [ ] FULL SUN [ ] PARTIAL SHADE [ ] MOSTLY SHADE [ ] FULL SHAD
WATER CROSSING: [ ] NONE [ ] ROCK HOP [ ] FOOTBRIDGE [ ] WET CROSSING

NUTRITION:

WATER: | **SNACKS:** | **MEALS:**

MAIN GEAR BROUGHT:

GEAR MISSED:

NOTES FOR NEXT TRIP:

BASICS

[ ] 1ST VISIT [ ] 2ND VISIT [ ] 3RD VISIT

DATE: / / LOCATION:

TRAIL:

| START TIME: :
END TIME: :
DURATION: | TEMP RANGE: | WEATHER:
☼ ⛅ ☁ ☂ 🌬 ❄ |

COMPANIONS:

FEES: PARKING/SHUTTLES:

BRIEF RECAP OF THE EXPERIENCE:

HIKE SPECIFICS [ ] COMPLETED [ ] NOT COMPLETED

TRAIL TYPE: [ ] LOOP [ ] OUT & BACK [ ] POINT TO POINT

DIFFICULTY: ☆☆☆☆☆ RATING: ☆☆☆☆☆

PRIMARY TERRAIN: [ ] DIRT [ ] ROCK [ ] PAVED [ ] OTHER:

ELEVATION: GAIN/LOSS:_____ START:_____ END:_____

SUITABILITY: [ ] DOG-FRIENDLY [ ] KID-FRIENDLY [ ] STROLLER-FRIENDLY
[ ] FULLY PAVED [ ] PARTIALLY PAVED [ ] WHEELCHAIR-FRIENDLY

TRAIL LENGTH:_____ COMPLETED: [ ] ALL [ ] OTHER: _____
TRAIL TRAFFIC: [ ] LIGHT [ ] MODERATE [ ] HEAVY
TRAIL ACTIVITIES: [ ] WALKING [ ] ROCK CLIMBING [ ] TRAIL RUNNING
[ ] MOUNTAIN BIKING [ ] BIRD WATCHING [ ] CAMPING
[ ] HORSEBACK RIDING [ ] OTHER: _____

SCENERY: [ ] NATURE VIEWS [ ] CITY VIEWS [ ] LAKE/RIVER [ ] WATERFALL
[ ] CLIFFS [ ] FOREST [ ] HISTORIC SITE [ ] HOT SPRINGS
[ ] WILD FLOWERS [ ] WILDLIFE [ ] OTHER: _____

EXPOSURE: [ ] NONE [ ] MINIMAL [ ] SOME [ ] EXTENSIVE

COVER/SHADE: [ ] FULL SUN [ ] PARTIAL SHADE [ ] MOSTLY SHADE [ ] FULL SHADE

WATER CROSSING: [ ] NONE [ ] ROCK HOP [ ] FOOTBRIDGE [ ] WET CROSSING

NUTRITION:

WATER: | **SNACKS:** | **MEALS:**

MAIN GEAR BROUGHT:

GEAR MISSED:

NOTES FOR NEXT TRIP:

BASICS

[ ] 1ST VISIT   [ ] 2ND VISIT   [ ] 3RD VISIT

DATE: /   /   LOCATION:

TRAIL:

START TIME: :   TEMP RANGE: WEATHER:
END TIME: :
DURATION:

COMPANIONS:

FEES: PARKING/SHUTTLES:

BRIEF RECAP OF THE EXPERIENCE:

HIKE SPECIFICS   [ ] COMPLETED   [ ] NOT COMPLETED

TRAIL TYPE: [ ] LOOP   [ ] OUT & BACK   [ ] POINT TO POINT

DIFFICULTY: ☆☆☆☆☆   RATING: ☆☆☆☆☆

PRIMARY TERRAIN: [ ] DIRT   [ ] ROCK [ ] PAVED [ ] OTHER:

ELEVATION: GAIN/LOSS:_____   START:_____ END:_____

SUITABILITY: [ ] DOG-FRIENDLY [ ] KID-FRIENDLY [ ] STROLLER-FRIENDLY
            [ ] FULLY PAVED [ ] PARTIALLY PAVED [ ] WHEELCHAIR-FRIENDLY

TRAIL LENGTH:_____ COMPLETED: [ ] ALL [ ] OTHER: _____
TRAIL TRAFFIC: [ ] LIGHT [ ] MODERATE [ ] HEAVY
TRAIL ACTIVITIES: [ ] WALKING   [ ] ROCK CLIMBING   [ ] TRAIL RUNNING
              [ ] MOUNTAIN BIKING [ ] BIRD WATCHING [ ] CAMPING
              [ ] HORSEBACK RIDING [ ] OTHER: _____

SCENERY: [ ] NATURE VIEWS [ ] CITY VIEWS [ ] LAKE/RIVER [ ] WATERFALL
          [ ] CLIFFS [ ] FOREST [ ] HISTORIC SITE [ ] HOT SPRINGS
          [ ] WILD FLOWERS [ ] WILDLIFE [ ] OTHER: _____

EXPOSURE: [ ] NONE [ ] MINIMAL [ ] SOME [ ] EXTENSIVE

COVER/SHADE: [ ] FULL SUN [ ] PARTIAL SHADE [ ] MOSTLY SHADE [ ] FULL SHADE

WATER CROSSING: [ ] NONE [ ] ROCK HOP [ ] FOOTBRIDGE [ ] WET CROSSING

NUTRITION:

WATER: | **SNACKS:** | **MEALS:**

MAIN GEAR BROUGHT:

GEAR MISSED:

NOTES FOR NEXT TRIP:

BASICS

[ ] 1ST VISIT [ ] 2ND VISIT [ ] 3RD VISIT

DATE: /   /   LOCATION:

TRAIL:

START TIME: :	TEMP RANGE:	WEATHER:
END TIME: :		☼ ☼ ☁ ☁ 🌬 ❄
DURATION:		

COMPANIONS:

FEES: PARKING/SHUTTLES:

BRIEF RECAP OF THE EXPERIENCE:

HIKE SPECIFICS [ ] COMPLETED   [ ] NOT COMPLETED

TRAIL TYPE: [ ] LOOP   [ ] OUT & BACK   [ ] POINT TO POINT

DIFFICULTY: ☆☆☆☆☆ RATING: ☆☆☆☆☆

PRIMARY TERRAIN: [ ] DIRT [ ] ROCK [ ] PAVED [ ] OTHER:

ELEVATION: GAIN/LOSS:_____ START:_____ END:_____

SUITABILITY: [ ] DOG-FRIENDLY [ ] KID-FRIENDLY [ ] STROLLER-FRIENDLY
             [ ] FULLY PAVED [ ] PARTIALLY PAVED [ ] WHEELCHAIR-FRIENDLY

TRAIL LENGTH:_____ COMPLETED: [ ] ALL [ ] OTHER: _____
TRAIL TRAFFIC: [ ] LIGHT [ ] MODERATE [ ] HEAVY
TRAIL ACTIVITIES: [ ] WALKING [ ] ROCK CLIMBING [ ] TRAIL RUNNING
                  [ ] MOUNTAIN BIKING [ ] BIRD WATCHING [ ] CAMPING
                  [ ] HORSEBACK RIDING [ ] OTHER: _____

SCENERY: [ ] NATURE VIEWS [ ] CITY VIEWS [ ] LAKE/RIVER [ ] WATERFALL
         [ ] CLIFFS [ ] FOREST [ ] HISTORIC SITE [ ] HOT SPRINGS
         [ ] WILD FLOWERS [ ] WILDLIFE [ ] OTHER: _____

EXPOSURE: [ ] NONE [ ] MINIMAL [ ] SOME [ ] EXTENSIVE

COVER/SHADE: [ ] FULL SUN [ ] PARTIAL SHADE [ ] MOSTLY SHADE [ ] FULL SHAD

WATER CROSSING: [ ] NONE [ ] ROCK HOP [ ] FOOTBRIDGE [ ] WET CROSSING

NUTRITION:

WATER: | **SNACKS:** | **MEALS:**

MAIN GEAR BROUGHT:

GEAR MISSED:

NOTES FOR NEXT TRIP:

BASICS

[ ] 1ST VISIT   [ ] 2ND VISIT   [ ] 3RD VISIT

DATE: /   /   LOCATION:

TRAIL:

START TIME: :   TEMP RANGE: WEATHER:
END TIME: :   ☀ 🌤 🌦 ☁ 🌬 ❄
DURATION:

COMPANIONS:

FEES: PARKING/SHUTTLES:

BRIEF RECAP OF THE EXPERIENCE:

HIKE SPECIFICS   [ ] COMPLETED   [ ] NOT COMPLETED

TRAIL TYPE: [ ] LOOP   [ ] OUT & BACK   [ ] POINT TO POINT

DIFFICULTY: ☆☆☆☆☆   RATING: ☆☆☆☆☆

PRIMARY TERRAIN: [ ] DIRT   [ ] ROCK   [ ] PAVED   [ ] OTHER:

ELEVATION: GAIN/LOSS:_____   START:_____   END:_____

SUITABILITY: [ ] DOG-FRIENDLY [ ] KID-FRIENDLY [ ] STROLLER-FRIENDLY
             [ ] FULLY PAVED [ ] PARTIALLY PAVED [ ] WHEELCHAIR-FRIENDLY

TRAIL LENGTH:_____ COMPLETED: [ ] ALL [ ] OTHER: _____
TRAIL TRAFFIC: [ ] LIGHT [ ] MODERATE [ ] HEAVY
TRAIL ACTIVITIES: [ ] WALKING   [ ] ROCK CLIMBING   [ ] TRAIL RUNNING
                  [ ] MOUNTAIN BIKING   [ ] BIRD WATCHING   [ ] CAMPING
                  [ ] HORSEBACK RIDING   [ ] OTHER: _____

SCENERY: [ ] NATURE VIEWS [ ] CITY VIEWS [ ] LAKE/RIVER [ ] WATERFALL
         [ ] CLIFFS [ ] FOREST [ ] HISTORIC SITE [ ] HOT SPRINGS
         [ ] WILD FLOWERS [ ] WILDLIFE [ ] OTHER: _____

EXPOSURE: [ ] NONE [ ] MINIMAL [ ] SOME [ ] EXTENSIVE

COVER/SHADE: [ ] FULL SUN [ ] PARTIAL SHADE [ ] MOSTLY SHADE [ ] FULL SHADE

WATER CROSSING: [ ] NONE [ ] ROCK HOP [ ] FOOTBRIDGE [ ] WET CROSSING

NUTRITION:

WATER: | **SNACKS:** | **MEALS:**

MAIN GEAR BROUGHT:

GEAR MISSED:

NOTES FOR NEXT TRIP:

BASICS

[ ] 1ST VISIT [ ] 2ND VISIT [ ] 3RD VISIT

DATE: /   /   LOCATION:

TRAIL:

START TIME: :	TEMP RANGE:	WEATHER:
END TIME: :		☀ ⛅ ⛈ 🌧 💨 ❄
DURATION:		

COMPANIONS:

FEES: PARKING/SHUTTLES:

BRIEF RECAP OF THE EXPERIENCE:

HIKE SPECIFICS [ ] COMPLETED   [ ] NOT COMPLETED

TRAIL TYPE: [ ] LOOP   [ ] OUT & BACK   [ ] POINT TO POINT

DIFFICULTY: ☆☆☆☆☆ RATING: ☆☆☆☆☆

PRIMARY TERRAIN: [ ] DIRT [ ] ROCK [ ] PAVED [ ] OTHER:

ELEVATION: GAIN/LOSS:_____ START:_____ END:_____

SUITABILITY: [ ] DOG-FRIENDLY [ ] KID-FRIENDLY [ ] STROLLER-FRIENDLY
[ ] FULLY PAVED [ ] PARTIALLY PAVED [ ] WHEELCHAIR-FRIENDLY

TRAIL LENGTH:_____ COMPLETED: [ ] ALL [ ] OTHER: _____
TRAIL TRAFFIC: [ ] LIGHT [ ] MODERATE [ ] HEAVY
TRAIL ACTIVITIES: [ ] WALKING [ ] ROCK CLIMBING [ ] TRAIL RUNNING
[ ] MOUNTAIN BIKING [ ] BIRD WATCHING [ ] CAMPING
[ ] HORSEBACK RIDING [ ] OTHER: _____

SCENERY: [ ] NATURE VIEWS [ ] CITY VIEWS [ ] LAKE/RIVER [ ] WATERFALL
[ ] CLIFFS [ ] FOREST [ ] HISTORIC SITE [ ] HOT SPRINGS
[ ] WILD FLOWERS [ ] WILDLIFE [ ] OTHER: _____

EXPOSURE: [ ] NONE [ ] MINIMAL [ ] SOME [ ] EXTENSIVE

COVER/SHADE: [ ] FULL SUN [ ] PARTIAL SHADE [ ] MOSTLY SHADE [ ] FULL SHADE

WATER CROSSING: [ ] NONE [ ] ROCK HOP [ ] FOOTBRIDGE [ ] WET CROSSING

NUTRITION:

WATER:	SNACKS:	MEALS:

MAIN GEAR BROUGHT:

GEAR MISSED:

NOTES FOR NEXT TRIP:

BASICS

[ ] 1ST VISIT [ ] 2ND VISIT [ ] 3RD VISIT

DATE: /   /   LOCATION:

TRAIL:

START TIME: :	TEMP RANGE:	WEATHER:
END TIME: :		☀ 🌤 ☁ 🌧 💨 ❄
DURATION:		

COMPANIONS:

FEES: PARKING/SHUTTLES:

BRIEF RECAP OF THE EXPERIENCE:

HIKE SPECIFICS [ ] COMPLETED   [ ] NOT COMPLETED

TRAIL TYPE: [ ] LOOP   [ ] OUT & BACK [ ] POINT TO POINT

DIFFICULTY: ☆☆☆☆☆ RATING: ☆☆☆☆☆

PRIMARY TERRAIN: [ ] DIRT [ ] ROCK [ ] PAVED [ ] OTHER:

ELEVATION: GAIN/LOSS:_____ START:_____ END:_____

SUITABILITY: [ ] DOG-FRIENDLY [ ] KID-FRIENDLY [ ] STROLLER-FRIENDLY
[ ] FULLY PAVED [ ] PARTIALLY PAVED [ ] WHEELCHAIR-FRIENDLY

TRAIL LENGTH:_____ COMPLETED: [ ] ALL [ ] OTHER: _____
TRAIL TRAFFIC: [ ] LIGHT [ ] MODERATE [ ] HEAVY
TRAIL ACTIVITIES: [ ] WALKING [ ] ROCK CLIMBING [ ] TRAIL RUNNING
[ ] MOUNTAIN BIKING [ ] BIRD WATCHING [ ] CAMPING
[ ] HORSEBACK RIDING [ ] OTHER: _____

SCENERY: [ ] NATURE VIEWS [ ] CITY VIEWS [ ] LAKE/RIVER [ ] WATERFALL
[ ] CLIFFS [ ] FOREST [ ] HISTORIC SITE [ ] HOT SPRINGS
[ ] WILD FLOWERS [ ] WILDLIFE [ ] OTHER: _____

EXPOSURE: [ ] NONE [ ] MINIMAL [ ] SOME [ ] EXTENSIVE

COVER/SHADE: [ ] FULL SUN [ ] PARTIAL SHADE [ ] MOSTLY SHADE [ ] FULL SHADE

WATER CROSSING: [ ] NONE [ ] ROCK HOP [ ] FOOTBRIDGE [ ] WET CROSSING

NUTRITION:

WATER: | **SNACKS:** | **MEALS:**

MAIN GEAR BROUGHT:

GEAR MISSED:

NOTES FOR NEXT TRIP:

BASICS

[ ] 1ST VISIT [ ] 2ND VISIT [ ] 3RD VISIT

DATE: /   /   LOCATION: _____

TRAIL: _____

START TIME: :	TEMP RANGE:	WEATHER:
END TIME: :		☀ ⛅ 🌦 🌧 💨 ❄
DURATION:		

COMPANIONS:

FEES: PARKING/SHUTTLES:

BRIEF RECAP OF THE EXPERIENCE:

HIKE SPECIFICS   [ ] COMPLETED   [ ] NOT COMPLETED

TRAIL TYPE: [ ] LOOP   [ ] OUT & BACK   [ ] POINT TO POINT

DIFFICULTY: ☆☆☆☆☆   RATING: ☆☆☆☆☆

PRIMARY TERRAIN: [ ] DIRT [ ] ROCK [ ] PAVED [ ] OTHER:

ELEVATION: GAIN/LOSS:_____ START:_____ END:_____

SUITABILITY: [ ] DOG-FRIENDLY [ ] KID-FRIENDLY [ ] STROLLER-FRIENDLY
             [ ] FULLY PAVED [ ] PARTIALLY PAVED [ ] WHEELCHAIR-FRIENDLY

TRAIL LENGTH:_____ COMPLETED: [ ] ALL [ ] OTHER: _____
TRAIL TRAFFIC: [ ] LIGHT [ ] MODERATE [ ] HEAVY
TRAIL ACTIVITIES: [ ] WALKING [ ] ROCK CLIMBING [ ] TRAIL RUNNING
                  [ ] MOUNTAIN BIKING [ ] BIRD WATCHING [ ] CAMPING
                  [ ] HORSEBACK RIDING [ ] OTHER: _____

SCENERY: [ ] NATURE VIEWS [ ] CITY VIEWS [ ] LAKE/RIVER [ ] WATERFALL
         [ ] CLIFFS [ ] FOREST [ ] HISTORIC SITE [ ] HOT SPRINGS
         [ ] WILD FLOWERS [ ] WILDLIFE [ ] OTHER: _____

EXPOSURE: [ ] NONE [ ] MINIMAL [ ] SOME [ ] EXTENSIVE

COVER/SHADE: [ ] FULL SUN [ ] PARTIAL SHADE [ ] MOSTLY SHADE [ ] FULL SHADE

WATER CROSSING: [ ] NONE [ ] ROCK HOP [ ] FOOTBRIDGE [ ] WET CROSSING

NUTRITION:

WATER: | **SNACKS:** | **MEALS:**

MAIN GEAR BROUGHT:

GEAR MISSED:

NOTES FOR NEXT TRIP:

BASICS

[ ] 1ST VISIT [ ] 2ND VISIT [ ] 3RD VISIT

DATE: / /   LOCATION:

TRAIL:

START TIME: :   TEMP RANGE: WEATHER:
END TIME: :
DURATION:

COMPANIONS:

FEES: PARKING/SHUTTLES:

BRIEF RECAP OF THE EXPERIENCE:

HIKE SPECIFICS [ ] COMPLETED   [ ] NOT COMPLETED

TRAIL TYPE: [ ] LOOP   [ ] OUT & BACK   [ ] POINT TO POINT

DIFFICULTY: ☆☆☆☆☆ RATING: ☆☆☆☆☆

PRIMARY TERRAIN: [ ] DIRT [ ] ROCK [ ] PAVED [ ] OTHER:

ELEVATION: GAIN/LOSS:_____ START:_____ END:_____

SUITABILITY: [ ] DOG-FRIENDLY [ ] KID-FRIENDLY [ ] STROLLER-FRIENDLY
            [ ] FULLY PAVED [ ] PARTIALLY PAVED [ ] WHEELCHAIR-FRIENDLY

TRAIL LENGTH:_____ COMPLETED: [ ] ALL [ ] OTHER: _____
TRAIL TRAFFIC: [ ] LIGHT [ ] MODERATE [ ] HEAVY
TRAIL ACTIVITIES: [ ] WALKING [ ] ROCK CLIMBING [ ] TRAIL RUNNING
                 [ ] MOUNTAIN BIKING [ ] BIRD WATCHING [ ] CAMPING
                 [ ] HORSEBACK RIDING [ ] OTHER: _____

SCENERY: [ ] NATURE VIEWS [ ] CITY VIEWS [ ] LAKE/RIVER [ ] WATERFALL
        [ ] CLIFFS [ ] FOREST [ ] HISTORIC SITE [ ] HOT SPRINGS
        [ ] WILD FLOWERS [ ] WILDLIFE [ ] OTHER: _____

EXPOSURE: [ ] NONE [ ] MINIMAL [ ] SOME [ ] EXTENSIVE

COVER/SHADE: [ ] FULL SUN [ ] PARTIAL SHADE [ ] MOSTLY SHADE [ ] FULL SHADE

WATER CROSSING: [ ] NONE [ ] ROCK HOP [ ] FOOTBRIDGE [ ] WET CROSSING

NUTRITION:

WATER: | **SNACKS:** | **MEALS:**

MAIN GEAR BROUGHT:

GEAR MISSED:

NOTES FOR NEXT TRIP:

BASICS

[ ] 1ST VISIT [ ] 2ND VISIT [ ] 3RD VISIT

DATE: /   /   LOCATION:

TRAIL:

START TIME: :   TEMP RANGE: WEATHER:
END TIME: :
DURATION:

COMPANIONS:

FEES: PARKING/SHUTTLES:

BRIEF RECAP OF THE EXPERIENCE:

HIKE SPECIFICS [ ] COMPLETED   [ ] NOT COMPLETED

TRAIL TYPE: [ ] LOOP   [ ] OUT & BACK   [ ] POINT TO POINT

DIFFICULTY: ☆☆☆☆☆ RATING: ☆☆☆☆☆

PRIMARY TERRAIN: [ ] DIRT [ ] ROCK [ ] PAVED [ ] OTHER:

ELEVATION: GAIN/LOSS:_____ START:_____ END:_____

SUITABILITY: [ ] DOG-FRIENDLY [ ] KID-FRIENDLY [ ] STROLLER-FRIENDLY
             [ ] FULLY PAVED [ ] PARTIALLY PAVED [ ] WHEELCHAIR-FRIENDLY

TRAIL LENGTH:_____ COMPLETED: [ ] ALL [ ] OTHER: _____
TRAIL TRAFFIC: [ ] LIGHT [ ] MODERATE [ ] HEAVY
TRAIL ACTIVITIES: [ ] WALKING [ ] ROCK CLIMBING [ ] TRAIL RUNNING
                 [ ] MOUNTAIN BIKING [ ] BIRD WATCHING [ ] CAMPING
                 [ ] HORSEBACK RIDING [ ] OTHER: _____

SCENERY: [ ] NATURE VIEWS [ ] CITY VIEWS [ ] LAKE/RIVER [ ] WATERFALL
         [ ] CLIFFS [ ] FOREST [ ] HISTORIC SITE [ ] HOT SPRINGS
         [ ] WILD FLOWERS [ ] WILDLIFE [ ] OTHER: _____

EXPOSURE: [ ] NONE [ ] MINIMAL [ ] SOME [ ] EXTENSIVE

COVER/SHADE: [ ] FULL SUN [ ] PARTIAL SHADE [ ] MOSTLY SHADE [ ] FULL SHAD

WATER CROSSING: [ ] NONE [ ] ROCK HOP [ ] FOOTBRIDGE [ ] WET CROSSING

NUTRITION:

WATER: | **SNACKS:** | **MEALS:**

MAIN GEAR BROUGHT:

GEAR MISSED:

NOTES FOR NEXT TRIP:

BASICS

[ ] 1ST VISIT   [ ] 2ND VISIT   [ ] 3RD VISIT

DATE: /   /   LOCATION:

TRAIL:

START TIME: :   TEMP RANGE: WEATHER:
END TIME: :
DURATION: ☼ ☼ ☁ ☁ ≈ ☁

COMPANIONS:

FEES: PARKING/SHUTTLES:

BRIEF RECAP OF THE EXPERIENCE:

HIKE SPECIFICS   [ ] COMPLETED   [ ] NOT COMPLETED

TRAIL TYPE: [ ] LOOP   [ ] OUT & BACK   [ ] POINT TO POINT

DIFFICULTY: ☆☆☆☆☆   RATING: ☆☆☆☆☆

PRIMARY TERRAIN: [ ] DIRT   [ ] ROCK   [ ] PAVED   [ ] OTHER:

ELEVATION: GAIN/LOSS:_____ START:_____ END:_____

SUITABILITY: [ ] DOG-FRIENDLY [ ] KID-FRIENDLY [ ] STROLLER-FRIENDLY
             [ ] FULLY PAVED [ ] PARTIALLY PAVED [ ] WHEELCHAIR-FRIENDLY

TRAIL LENGTH:_____ COMPLETED: [ ] ALL [ ] OTHER: _____
TRAIL TRAFFIC: [ ] LIGHT [ ] MODERATE [ ] HEAVY
TRAIL ACTIVITIES: [ ] WALKING   [ ] ROCK CLIMBING [ ] TRAIL RUNNING
                  [ ] MOUNTAIN BIKING [ ] BIRD WATCHING [ ] CAMPING
                  [ ] HORSEBACK RIDING [ ] OTHER: _____

SCENERY: [ ] NATURE VIEWS [ ] CITY VIEWS [ ] LAKE/RIVER [ ] WATERFALL
         [ ] CLIFFS [ ] FOREST [ ] HISTORIC SITE [ ] HOT SPRINGS
         [ ] WILD FLOWERS [ ] WILDLIFE [ ] OTHER: _____

EXPOSURE: [ ] NONE [ ] MINIMAL [ ] SOME [ ] EXTENSIVE

COVER/SHADE: [ ] FULL SUN [ ] PARTIAL SHADE [ ] MOSTLY SHADE [ ] FULL SHADE

WATER CROSSING: [ ] NONE [ ] ROCK HOP [ ] FOOTBRIDGE [ ] WET CROSSING

NUTRITION:

WATER: | **SNACKS:** | **MEALS:**

MAIN GEAR BROUGHT:

GEAR MISSED:

NOTES FOR NEXT TRIP:

BASICS

[ ] 1ST VISIT   [ ] 2ND VISIT   [ ] 3RD VISIT

DATE: /   /   LOCATION:

TRAIL:

START TIME: :	TEMP RANGE:	WEATHER:
END TIME: :		☀ ⛅ 🌦 ☁ 🌬 🌨
DURATION:		

COMPANIONS:

FEES: PARKING/SHUTTLES:

BRIEF RECAP OF THE EXPERIENCE:

HIKE SPECIFICS   [ ] COMPLETED   [ ] NOT COMPLETED

TRAIL TYPE: [ ] LOOP   [ ] OUT & BACK   [ ] POINT TO POINT

DIFFICULTY: ☆☆☆☆☆   RATING: ☆☆☆☆☆

PRIMARY TERRAIN: [ ] DIRT   [ ] ROCK   [ ] PAVED   [ ] OTHER:

ELEVATION: GAIN/LOSS:_____ START:_____ END:_____

SUITABILITY: [ ] DOG-FRIENDLY [ ] KID-FRIENDLY [ ] STROLLER-FRIENDLY
             [ ] FULLY PAVED [ ] PARTIALLY PAVED [ ] WHEELCHAIR-FRIENDLY

TRAIL LENGTH:_____ COMPLETED: [ ] ALL [ ] OTHER: _____
TRAIL TRAFFIC: [ ] LIGHT [ ] MODERATE [ ] HEAVY
TRAIL ACTIVITIES: [ ] WALKING [ ] ROCK CLIMBING [ ] TRAIL RUNNING
                  [ ] MOUNTAIN BIKING [ ] BIRD WATCHING [ ] CAMPING
                  [ ] HORSEBACK RIDING [ ] OTHER: _____

SCENERY: [ ] NATURE VIEWS [ ] CITY VIEWS [ ] LAKE/RIVER [ ] WATERFALL
         [ ] CLIFFS [ ] FOREST [ ] HISTORIC SITE [ ] HOT SPRINGS
         [ ] WILD FLOWERS [ ] WILDLIFE [ ] OTHER: _____

EXPOSURE: [ ] NONE [ ] MINIMAL [ ] SOME [ ] EXTENSIVE

COVER/SHADE: [ ] FULL SUN [ ] PARTIAL SHADE [ ] MOSTLY SHADE [ ] FULL SHADE

WATER CROSSING: [ ] NONE [ ] ROCK HOP [ ] FOOTBRIDGE [ ] WET CROSSING

NUTRITION:

WATER: | **SNACKS:** | **MEALS:**

MAIN GEAR BROUGHT:

GEAR MISSED:

NOTES FOR NEXT TRIP:

BASICS

[ ] 1ST VISIT [ ] 2ND VISIT [ ] 3RD VISIT

DATE: /   /   LOCATION:

TRAIL:

START TIME: :   TEMP RANGE: WEATHER:
END TIME: :
DURATION: ☀ ⛅ ⛈ ☁ 🌬 ❄

COMPANIONS:

FEES: PARKING/SHUTTLES:

BRIEF RECAP OF THE EXPERIENCE:

HIKE SPECIFICS [ ] COMPLETED   [ ] NOT COMPLETED

TRAIL TYPE: [ ] LOOP   [ ] OUT & BACK [ ] POINT TO POINT

DIFFICULTY: ☆☆☆☆☆ RATING: ☆☆☆☆☆

PRIMARY TERRAIN: [ ] DIRT [ ] ROCK [ ] PAVED [ ] OTHER:

ELEVATION: GAIN/LOSS:_____ START:_____ END:_____

SUITABILITY: [ ] DOG-FRIENDLY [ ] KID-FRIENDLY [ ] STROLLER-FRIENDLY
[ ] FULLY PAVED [ ] PARTIALLY PAVED [ ] WHEELCHAIR-FRIENDLY

TRAIL LENGTH:_____ COMPLETED: [ ] ALL [ ] OTHER: _____
TRAIL TRAFFIC: [ ] LIGHT [ ] MODERATE [ ] HEAVY
TRAIL ACTIVITIES: [ ] WALKING [ ] ROCK CLIMBING [ ] TRAIL RUNNING
[ ] MOUNTAIN BIKING [ ] BIRD WATCHING [ ] CAMPING
[ ] HORSEBACK RIDING [ ] OTHER: _____

SCENERY: [ ] NATURE VIEWS [ ] CITY VIEWS [ ] LAKE/RIVER [ ] WATERFALL
[ ] CLIFFS [ ] FOREST [ ] HISTORIC SITE [ ] HOT SPRINGS
[ ] WILD FLOWERS [ ] WILDLIFE [ ] OTHER: _____

EXPOSURE: [ ] NONE [ ] MINIMAL [ ] SOME [ ] EXTENSIVE

COVER/SHADE: [ ] FULL SUN [ ] PARTIAL SHADE [ ] MOSTLY SHADE [ ] FULL SHAD

WATER CROSSING: [ ] NONE [ ] ROCK HOP [ ] FOOTBRIDGE [ ] WET CROSSING

NUTRITION:

WATER: | **SNACKS:** | **MEALS:**

MAIN GEAR BROUGHT:

GEAR MISSED:

NOTES FOR NEXT TRIP:

BASICS

[ ] 1ST VISIT [ ] 2ND VISIT [ ] 3RD VISIT

DATE: / /   LOCATION:

TRAIL:

START TIME: :   TEMP RANGE: WEATHER:
END TIME: :
DURATION:

COMPANIONS:

FEES: PARKING/SHUTTLES:

BRIEF RECAP OF THE EXPERIENCE:

HIKE SPECIFICS [ ] COMPLETED   [ ] NOT COMPLETED

TRAIL TYPE: [ ] LOOP   [ ] OUT & BACK   [ ] POINT TO POINT

DIFFICULTY: ☆☆☆☆☆ RATING: ☆☆☆☆☆

PRIMARY TERRAIN: [ ] DIRT [ ] ROCK [ ] PAVED [ ] OTHER:

ELEVATION: GAIN/LOSS:_____ START:_____ END:_____

SUITABILITY: [ ] DOG-FRIENDLY [ ] KID-FRIENDLY [ ] STROLLER-FRIENDLY
     [ ] FULLY PAVED [ ] PARTIALLY PAVED [ ] WHEELCHAIR-FRIENDLY

TRAIL LENGTH:_____ COMPLETED: [ ] ALL [ ] OTHER: _____
TRAIL TRAFFIC: [ ] LIGHT [ ] MODERATE [ ] HEAVY
TRAIL ACTIVITIES: [ ] WALKING [ ] ROCK CLIMBING [ ] TRAIL RUNNING
     [ ] MOUNTAIN BIKING [ ] BIRD WATCHING [ ] CAMPING
     [ ] HORSEBACK RIDING [ ] OTHER: _____

SCENERY: [ ] NATURE VIEWS [ ] CITY VIEWS [ ] LAKE/RIVER [ ] WATERFALL
    [ ] CLIFFS [ ] FOREST [ ] HISTORIC SITE [ ] HOT SPRINGS
    [ ] WILD FLOWERS [ ] WILDLIFE [ ] OTHER: _____

EXPOSURE: [ ] NONE [ ] MINIMAL [ ] SOME [ ] EXTENSIVE

COVER/SHADE: [ ] FULL SUN [ ] PARTIAL SHADE [ ] MOSTLY SHADE [ ] FULL SHADE

WATER CROSSING: [ ] NONE [ ] ROCK HOP [ ] FOOTBRIDGE [ ] WET CROSSING

NUTRITION:

WATER:	SNACKS:	MEALS:

MAIN GEAR BROUGHT:

GEAR MISSED:

NOTES FOR NEXT TRIP:

BASICS

[ ] 1ST VISIT [ ] 2ND VISIT [ ] 3RD VISIT

DATE: /   /   LOCATION:

TRAIL:

START TIME: :	TEMP RANGE:	WEATHER:
END TIME: :		☼ ☼ ☼ ☁ 〜 ❄
DURATION:		

COMPANIONS:

FEES: PARKING/SHUTTLES:

BRIEF RECAP OF THE EXPERIENCE:

HIKE SPECIFICS [ ] COMPLETED   [ ] NOT COMPLETED

TRAIL TYPE: [ ] LOOP   [ ] OUT & BACK   [ ] POINT TO POINT

DIFFICULTY: ☆☆☆☆☆ RATING: ☆☆☆☆☆

PRIMARY TERRAIN:[ ] DIRT [ ] ROCK [ ] PAVED [ ] OTHER:

ELEVATION: GAIN/LOSS:_____ START:_____ END:_____

SUITABILITY:[ ] DOG-FRIENDLY [ ] KID-FRIENDLY [ ] STROLLER-FRIENDLY
          [ ] FULLY PAVED [ ] PARTIALLY PAVED [ ] WHEELCHAIR-FRIENDLY

TRAIL LENGTH:_____ COMPLETED: [ ] ALL [ ] OTHER: _____
TRAIL TRAFFIC: [ ] LIGHT [ ] MODERATE [ ] HEAVY
TRAIL ACTIVITIES: [ ] WALKING [ ] ROCK CLIMBING [ ] TRAIL RUNNING
               [ ] MOUNTAIN BIKING [ ] BIRD WATCHING [ ] CAMPING
               [ ] HORSEBACK RIDING [ ] OTHER: _____

SCENERY: [ ] NATURE VIEWS [ ] CITY VIEWS [ ] LAKE/RIVER [ ] WATERFALL
        [ ] CLIFFS [ ] FOREST [ ] HISTORIC SITE [ ] HOT SPRINGS
        [ ] WILD FLOWERS [ ] WILDLIFE [ ] OTHER: _____

EXPOSURE: [ ] NONE [ ] MINIMAL [ ] SOME [ ] EXTENSIVE

COVER/SHADE: [ ] FULL SUN [ ] PARTIAL SHADE [ ] MOSTLY SHADE [ ] FULL SHADE

WATER CROSSING: [ ] NONE [ ] ROCK HOP [ ] FOOTBRIDGE [ ] WET CROSSING

NUTRITION:

WATER: | **SNACKS:** | **MEALS:**

MAIN GEAR BROUGHT:

GEAR MISSED:

NOTES FOR NEXT TRIP:

BASICS

[ ] 1ST VISIT [ ] 2ND VISIT [ ] 3RD VISIT

DATE: /   /   LOCATION:

TRAIL:

START TIME: :	TEMP RANGE:	WEATHER:
END TIME: :		☀ ⛅ ⛅ ☁ 🌬 ❄
DURATION:		

COMPANIONS:

FEES: PARKING/SHUTTLES:

BRIEF RECAP OF THE EXPERIENCE:

HIKE SPECIFICS [ ] COMPLETED   [ ] NOT COMPLETED

TRAIL TYPE: [ ] LOOP   [ ] OUT & BACK [ ] POINT TO POINT

DIFFICULTY: ☆☆☆☆☆ RATING: ☆☆☆☆☆

PRIMARY TERRAIN: [ ] DIRT [ ] ROCK [ ] PAVED [ ] OTHER:

ELEVATION: GAIN/LOSS:_____ START:_____ END:_____

SUITABILITY: [ ] DOG-FRIENDLY [ ] KID-FRIENDLY [ ] STROLLER-FRIENDLY
[ ] FULLY PAVED [ ] PARTIALLY PAVED [ ] WHEELCHAIR-FRIENDLY

TRAIL LENGTH:_____ COMPLETED: [ ] ALL [ ] OTHER: _____

TRAIL TRAFFIC: [ ] LIGHT [ ] MODERATE [ ] HEAVY

TRAIL ACTIVITIES: [ ] WALKING [ ] ROCK CLIMBING [ ] TRAIL RUNNING
[ ] MOUNTAIN BIKING [ ] BIRD WATCHING [ ] CAMPING
[ ] HORSEBACK RIDING [ ] OTHER: _____

SCENERY: [ ] NATURE VIEWS [ ] CITY VIEWS [ ] LAKE/RIVER [ ] WATERFALL
[ ] CLIFFS [ ] FOREST [ ] HISTORIC SITE [ ] HOT SPRINGS
[ ] WILD FLOWERS [ ] WILDLIFE [ ] OTHER: _____

EXPOSURE: [ ] NONE [ ] MINIMAL [ ] SOME [ ] EXTENSIVE

COVER/SHADE: [ ] FULL SUN [ ] PARTIAL SHADE [ ] MOSTLY SHADE [ ] FULL SHADE

WATER CROSSING: [ ] NONE [ ] ROCK HOP [ ] FOOTBRIDGE [ ] WET CROSSING

NUTRITION:

WATER: | **SNACKS:** | **MEALS:**

MAIN GEAR BROUGHT:

GEAR MISSED:

NOTES FOR NEXT TRIP:

BASICS

[ ] 1ST VISIT [ ] 2ND VISIT [ ] 3RD VISIT

DATE: /   /   LOCATION:

TRAIL:

START TIME: :
END TIME: :
DURATION:

TEMP RANGE:

WEATHER:
☀ ⛅ 🌦 🌧 🌬 🌨

COMPANIONS:

FEES: PARKING/SHUTTLES:

BRIEF RECAP OF THE EXPERIENCE:

HIKE SPECIFICS [ ] COMPLETED   [ ] NOT COMPLETED

TRAIL TYPE: [ ] LOOP   [ ] OUT & BACK   [ ] POINT TO POINT

DIFFICULTY: ☆☆☆☆☆ RATING: ☆☆☆☆☆

PRIMARY TERRAIN: [ ] DIRT [ ] ROCK [ ] PAVED [ ] OTHER:

ELEVATION: GAIN/LOSS:_____ START:_____ END:_____

SUITABILITY: [ ] DOG-FRIENDLY [ ] KID-FRIENDLY [ ] STROLLER-FRIENDLY
             [ ] FULLY PAVED [ ] PARTIALLY PAVED [ ] WHEELCHAIR-FRIENDLY

TRAIL LENGTH:_____ COMPLETED: [ ] ALL [ ] OTHER: _____
TRAIL TRAFFIC: [ ] LIGHT [ ] MODERATE [ ] HEAVY
TRAIL ACTIVITIES: [ ] WALKING [ ] ROCK CLIMBING [ ] TRAIL RUNNING
                  [ ] MOUNTAIN BIKING [ ] BIRD WATCHING [ ] CAMPING
                  [ ] HORSEBACK RIDING [ ] OTHER: _____

SCENERY: [ ] NATURE VIEWS [ ] CITY VIEWS [ ] LAKE/RIVER [ ] WATERFALL
         [ ] CLIFFS [ ] FOREST [ ] HISTORIC SITE [ ] HOT SPRINGS
         [ ] WILD FLOWERS [ ] WILDLIFE [ ] OTHER: _____

EXPOSURE: [ ] NONE [ ] MINIMAL [ ] SOME [ ] EXTENSIVE

COVER/SHADE: [ ] FULL SUN [ ] PARTIAL SHADE [ ] MOSTLY SHADE [ ] FULL SHADE

WATER CROSSING: [ ] NONE [ ] ROCK HOP [ ] FOOTBRIDGE [ ] WET CROSSING

NUTRITION:

WATER: | **SNACKS:** | **MEALS:**

MAIN GEAR BROUGHT:

GEAR MISSED:

NOTES FOR NEXT TRIP:

BASICS

[ ] 1ST VISIT [ ] 2ND VISIT [ ] 3RD VISIT

DATE: /   /   LOCATION:

TRAIL:

START TIME: :	TEMP RANGE:	WEATHER:
END TIME: :		☀️ 🌤️ 🌦️ 🌧️ 🌬️ 🌨️
DURATION:		

COMPANIONS:

FEES: PARKING/SHUTTLES:

BRIEF RECAP OF THE EXPERIENCE:

HIKE SPECIFICS [ ] COMPLETED   [ ] NOT COMPLETED

TRAIL TYPE: [ ] LOOP   [ ] OUT & BACK   [ ] POINT TO POINT

DIFFICULTY: ☆☆☆☆☆ RATING: ☆☆☆☆☆

PRIMARY TERRAIN: [ ] DIRT [ ] ROCK [ ] PAVED [ ] OTHER:

ELEVATION: GAIN/LOSS:_____ START:_____ END:_____

SUITABILITY: [ ] DOG-FRIENDLY [ ] KID-FRIENDLY [ ] STROLLER-FRIENDLY
            [ ] FULLY PAVED [ ] PARTIALLY PAVED [ ] WHEELCHAIR-FRIENDLY

TRAIL LENGTH:_____ COMPLETED: [ ] ALL [ ] OTHER: _____
TRAIL TRAFFIC: [ ] LIGHT [ ] MODERATE [ ] HEAVY
TRAIL ACTIVITIES: [ ] WALKING [ ] ROCK CLIMBING [ ] TRAIL RUNNING
                 [ ] MOUNTAIN BIKING [ ] BIRD WATCHING [ ] CAMPING
                 [ ] HORSEBACK RIDING [ ] OTHER: _____

SCENERY: [ ] NATURE VIEWS [ ] CITY VIEWS [ ] LAKE/RIVER [ ] WATERFALL
         [ ] CLIFFS [ ] FOREST [ ] HISTORIC SITE [ ] HOT SPRINGS
         [ ] WILD FLOWERS [ ] WILDLIFE [ ] OTHER: _____

EXPOSURE: [ ] NONE [ ] MINIMAL [ ] SOME [ ] EXTENSIVE

COVER/SHADE: [ ] FULL SUN [ ] PARTIAL SHADE [ ] MOSTLY SHADE [ ] FULL SHADE

WATER CROSSING: [ ] NONE [ ] ROCK HOP [ ] FOOTBRIDGE [ ] WET CROSSING

NUTRITION:

WATER:

SNACKS:

MEALS:

MAIN GEAR BROUGHT:

GEAR MISSED:

NOTES FOR NEXT TRIP:

BASICS

[ ] 1ST VISIT [ ] 2ND VISIT [ ] 3RD VISIT

DATE: /   /   LOCATION:

TRAIL:

START TIME: :	TEMP RANGE:	WEATHER:
END TIME: :		
DURATION:		☀ ⛅ 🌤 ☁ 🌬 ❄

COMPANIONS:

FEES: PARKING/SHUTTLES:

BRIEF RECAP OF THE EXPERIENCE:

HIKE SPECIFICS [ ] COMPLETED   [ ] NOT COMPLETED

TRAIL TYPE: [ ] LOOP   [ ] OUT & BACK [ ] POINT TO POINT

DIFFICULTY: ☆☆☆☆☆ RATING: ☆☆☆☆☆

PRIMARY TERRAIN:[ ] DIRT [ ] ROCK [ ] PAVED [ ] OTHER:

ELEVATION: GAIN/LOSS:_____ START:_____ END:_____

SUITABILITY: [ ] DOG-FRIENDLY [ ] KID-FRIENDLY [ ] STROLLER-FRIENDLY
[ ] FULLY PAVED [ ] PARTIALLY PAVED [ ] WHEELCHAIR-FRIENDLY

TRAIL LENGTH:_____ COMPLETED: [ ] ALL [ ] OTHER: _____
TRAIL TRAFFIC: [ ] LIGHT [ ] MODERATE [ ] HEAVY
TRAIL ACTIVITIES: [ ] WALKING [ ] ROCK CLIMBING [ ] TRAIL RUNNING
[ ] MOUNTAIN BIKING [ ] BIRD WATCHING [ ] CAMPING
[ ] HORSEBACK RIDING [ ] OTHER: _____

SCENERY: [ ] NATURE VIEWS [ ] CITY VIEWS [ ] LAKE/RIVER [ ] WATERFALL
[ ] CLIFFS [ ] FOREST [ ] HISTORIC SITE [ ] HOT SPRINGS
[ ] WILD FLOWERS [ ] WILDLIFE [ ] OTHER: _____

EXPOSURE: [ ] NONE [ ] MINIMAL [ ] SOME [ ] EXTENSIVE

COVER/SHADE: [ ] FULL SUN [ ] PARTIAL SHADE [ ] MOSTLY SHADE [ ] FULL SHAD

WATER CROSSING: [ ] NONE [ ] ROCK HOP [ ] FOOTBRIDGE [ ] WET CROSSING

NUTRITION:

WATER: | **SNACKS:** | **MEALS:**

MAIN GEAR BROUGHT:

GEAR MISSED:

NOTES FOR NEXT TRIP:

BASICS

[ ] 1ST VISIT [ ] 2ND VISIT [ ] 3RD VISIT

DATE: /   /   LOCATION:

TRAIL:

START TIME: :	TEMP RANGE:	WEATHER:
END TIME: :		☼ ⛅ 🌦 🌧 💨 ❄
DURATION:		

COMPANIONS:

FEES: PARKING/SHUTTLES:

BRIEF RECAP OF THE EXPERIENCE:

HIKE SPECIFICS   [ ] COMPLETED   [ ] NOT COMPLETED

TRAIL TYPE: [ ] LOOP   [ ] OUT & BACK   [ ] POINT TO POINT

DIFFICULTY: ☆☆☆☆☆   RATING: ☆☆☆☆☆

PRIMARY TERRAIN: [ ] DIRT [ ] ROCK [ ] PAVED [ ] OTHER:

ELEVATION: GAIN/LOSS:_____ START:_____ END:_____

SUITABILITY: [ ] DOG-FRIENDLY [ ] KID-FRIENDLY [ ] STROLLER-FRIENDLY
         [ ] FULLY PAVED [ ] PARTIALLY PAVED [ ] WHEELCHAIR-FRIENDLY

TRAIL LENGTH:_____ COMPLETED: [ ] ALL [ ] OTHER: _____
TRAIL TRAFFIC: [ ] LIGHT [ ] MODERATE [ ] HEAVY
TRAIL ACTIVITIES: [ ] WALKING [ ] ROCK CLIMBING [ ] TRAIL RUNNING
             [ ] MOUNTAIN BIKING [ ] BIRD WATCHING [ ] CAMPING
             [ ] HORSEBACK RIDING [ ] OTHER: _____

SCENERY: [ ] NATURE VIEWS [ ] CITY VIEWS [ ] LAKE/RIVER [ ] WATERFALL
       [ ] CLIFFS [ ] FOREST [ ] HISTORIC SITE [ ] HOT SPRINGS
       [ ] WILD FLOWERS [ ] WILDLIFE [ ] OTHER: _____

EXPOSURE: [ ] NONE [ ] MINIMAL [ ] SOME [ ] EXTENSIVE

COVER/SHADE: [ ] FULL SUN [ ] PARTIAL SHADE [ ] MOSTLY SHADE [ ] FULL SHADE

WATER CROSSING: [ ] NONE [ ] ROCK HOP [ ] FOOTBRIDGE [ ] WET CROSSING

NUTRITION:

WATER: | **SNACKS:** | **MEALS:**

MAIN GEAR BROUGHT:

GEAR MISSED:

NOTES FOR NEXT TRIP:

BASICS

[ ] 1ST VISIT [ ] 2ND VISIT [ ] 3RD VISIT

DATE: / / LOCATION:

TRAIL:

START TIME: :	TEMP RANGE:	WEATHER:
END TIME: :		☀ ⛅ 🌦 🌧 💨 ❄
DURATION:		

COMPANIONS:

FEES: PARKING/SHUTTLES:

BRIEF RECAP OF THE EXPERIENCE:

HIKE SPECIFICS [ ] COMPLETED [ ] NOT COMPLETED

TRAIL TYPE: [ ] LOOP [ ] OUT & BACK [ ] POINT TO POINT

DIFFICULTY: ☆☆☆☆☆ RATING: ☆☆☆☆☆

PRIMARY TERRAIN: [ ] DIRT [ ] ROCK [ ] PAVED [ ] OTHER:

ELEVATION: GAIN/LOSS:_____ START:_____ END:_____

SUITABILITY: [ ] DOG-FRIENDLY [ ] KID-FRIENDLY [ ] STROLLER-FRIENDLY
[ ] FULLY PAVED [ ] PARTIALLY PAVED [ ] WHEELCHAIR-FRIENDLY

TRAIL LENGTH:_____ COMPLETED: [ ] ALL [ ] OTHER: _____
TRAIL TRAFFIC: [ ] LIGHT [ ] MODERATE [ ] HEAVY
TRAIL ACTIVITIES: [ ] WALKING [ ] ROCK CLIMBING [ ] TRAIL RUNNING
[ ] MOUNTAIN BIKING [ ] BIRD WATCHING [ ] CAMPING
[ ] HORSEBACK RIDING [ ] OTHER: _____

SCENERY: [ ] NATURE VIEWS [ ] CITY VIEWS [ ] LAKE/RIVER [ ] WATERFALL
[ ] CLIFFS [ ] FOREST [ ] HISTORIC SITE [ ] HOT SPRINGS
[ ] WILD FLOWERS [ ] WILDLIFE [ ] OTHER: _____

EXPOSURE: [ ] NONE [ ] MINIMAL [ ] SOME [ ] EXTENSIVE

COVER/SHADE: [ ] FULL SUN [ ] PARTIAL SHADE [ ] MOSTLY SHADE [ ] FULL SHADE

WATER CROSSING: [ ] NONE [ ] ROCK HOP [ ] FOOTBRIDGE [ ] WET CROSSING

NUTRITION:

WATER: | **SNACKS:** | **MEALS:**

MAIN GEAR BROUGHT:

GEAR MISSED:

NOTES FOR NEXT TRIP:

BASICS

[ ] 1ST VISIT [ ] 2ND VISIT [ ] 3RD VISIT

DATE: / / LOCATION:

TRAIL:

START TIME: : | TEMP RANGE: | WEATHER:
END TIME: :
DURATION:

COMPANIONS:

FEES: PARKING/SHUTTLES:

BRIEF RECAP OF THE EXPERIENCE:

HIKE SPECIFICS [ ] COMPLETED [ ] NOT COMPLETED

TRAIL TYPE: [ ] LOOP [ ] OUT & BACK [ ] POINT TO POINT

DIFFICULTY: ☆☆☆☆☆ RATING: ☆☆☆☆☆

PRIMARY TERRAIN: [ ] DIRT [ ] ROCK [ ] PAVED [ ] OTHER:

ELEVATION: GAIN/LOSS:_____ START:_____ END:_____

SUITABILITY: [ ] DOG-FRIENDLY [ ] KID-FRIENDLY [ ] STROLLER-FRIENDLY
[ ] FULLY PAVED [ ] PARTIALLY PAVED [ ] WHEELCHAIR-FRIENDLY

TRAIL LENGTH:_____ COMPLETED: [ ] ALL [ ] OTHER: _____

TRAIL TRAFFIC: [ ] LIGHT [ ] MODERATE [ ] HEAVY

TRAIL ACTIVITIES: [ ] WALKING [ ] ROCK CLIMBING [ ] TRAIL RUNNING
[ ] MOUNTAIN BIKING [ ] BIRD WATCHING [ ] CAMPING
[ ] HORSEBACK RIDING [ ] OTHER: _____

SCENERY: [ ] NATURE VIEWS [ ] CITY VIEWS [ ] LAKE/RIVER [ ] WATERFALL
[ ] CLIFFS [ ] FOREST [ ] HISTORIC SITE [ ] HOT SPRINGS
[ ] WILD FLOWERS [ ] WILDLIFE [ ] OTHER: _____

EXPOSURE: [ ] NONE [ ] MINIMAL [ ] SOME [ ] EXTENSIVE

COVER/SHADE: [ ] FULL SUN [ ] PARTIAL SHADE [ ] MOSTLY SHADE [ ] FULL SHAD

WATER CROSSING: [ ] NONE [ ] ROCK HOP [ ] FOOTBRIDGE [ ] WET CROSSING

NUTRITION:

WATER: | **SNACKS:** | **MEALS:**

MAIN GEAR BROUGHT:

GEAR MISSED:

NOTES FOR NEXT TRIP:

BASICS

[ ] 1ST VISIT [ ] 2ND VISIT [ ] 3RD VISIT

DATE: /   /   LOCATION:

TRAIL:

START TIME: : | TEMP RANGE: | WEATHER:
END TIME: : | | ☀ ⛅ 🌦 ☁ 🌬 ❄
DURATION: | |

COMPANIONS:

FEES: PARKING/SHUTTLES:

BRIEF RECAP OF THE EXPERIENCE:

HIKE SPECIFICS [ ] COMPLETED   [ ] NOT COMPLETED

TRAIL TYPE: [ ] LOOP   [ ] OUT & BACK   [ ] POINT TO POINT

DIFFICULTY: ☆☆☆☆☆ RATING: ☆☆☆☆☆

PRIMARY TERRAIN: [ ] DIRT [ ] ROCK [ ] PAVED [ ] OTHER:

ELEVATION: GAIN/LOSS:_____ START:_____ END:_____

SUITABILITY: [ ] DOG-FRIENDLY [ ] KID-FRIENDLY [ ] STROLLER-FRIENDLY
             [ ] FULLY PAVED [ ] PARTIALLY PAVED [ ] WHEELCHAIR-FRIENDLY

TRAIL LENGTH:_____ COMPLETED: [ ] ALL [ ] OTHER: _____
TRAIL TRAFFIC: [ ] LIGHT [ ] MODERATE [ ] HEAVY
TRAIL ACTIVITIES: [ ] WALKING [ ] ROCK CLIMBING [ ] TRAIL RUNNING
                  [ ] MOUNTAIN BIKING [ ] BIRD WATCHING [ ] CAMPING
                  [ ] HORSEBACK RIDING [ ] OTHER: _____

SCENERY: [ ] NATURE VIEWS [ ] CITY VIEWS [ ] LAKE/RIVER [ ] WATERFALL
         [ ] CLIFFS [ ] FOREST [ ] HISTORIC SITE [ ] HOT SPRINGS
         [ ] WILD FLOWERS [ ] WILDLIFE [ ] OTHER: _____

EXPOSURE: [ ] NONE [ ] MINIMAL [ ] SOME [ ] EXTENSIVE

COVER/SHADE: [ ] FULL SUN [ ] PARTIAL SHADE [ ] MOSTLY SHADE [ ] FULL SHADE

WATER CROSSING: [ ] NONE [ ] ROCK HOP [ ] FOOTBRIDGE [ ] WET CROSSING

NUTRITION:

WATER: | **SNACKS:** | **MEALS:**

MAIN GEAR BROUGHT:

GEAR MISSED:

NOTES FOR NEXT TRIP:

BASICS

[ ] 1ST VISIT   [ ] 2ND VISIT   [ ] 3RD VISIT

DATE: /   /   LOCATION:

TRAIL:

| START TIME: :
END TIME: :
DURATION: | TEMP RANGE: | WEATHER:
☀ 🌤 ⛅ ☁ 🌬 🌨 |

COMPANIONS:

FEES: PARKING/SHUTTLES:

BRIEF RECAP OF THE EXPERIENCE:

HIKE SPECIFICS   [ ] COMPLETED   [ ] NOT COMPLETED

TRAIL TYPE: [ ] LOOP   [ ] OUT & BACK   [ ] POINT TO POINT

DIFFICULTY: ☆☆☆☆☆   RATING: ☆☆☆☆☆

PRIMARY TERRAIN: [ ] DIRT   [ ] ROCK   [ ] PAVED   [ ] OTHER:

ELEVATION: GAIN/LOSS:_____   START:_____ END:_____

SUITABILITY: [ ] DOG-FRIENDLY [ ] KID-FRIENDLY [ ] STROLLER-FRIENDLY
[ ] FULLY PAVED [ ] PARTIALLY PAVED [ ] WHEELCHAIR-FRIENDLY

TRAIL LENGTH:_____ COMPLETED: [ ] ALL [ ] OTHER: _____
TRAIL TRAFFIC: [ ] LIGHT [ ] MODERATE [ ] HEAVY
TRAIL ACTIVITIES: [ ] WALKING   [ ] ROCK CLIMBING   [ ] TRAIL RUNNING
[ ] MOUNTAIN BIKING [ ] BIRD WATCHING [ ] CAMPING
[ ] HORSEBACK RIDING [ ] OTHER: _____

SCENERY: [ ] NATURE VIEWS [ ] CITY VIEWS [ ] LAKE/RIVER [ ] WATERFALL
[ ] CLIFFS [ ] FOREST [ ] HISTORIC SITE [ ] HOT SPRINGS
[ ] WILD FLOWERS [ ] WILDLIFE [ ] OTHER: _____

EXPOSURE: [ ] NONE [ ] MINIMAL [ ] SOME [ ] EXTENSIVE

COVER/SHADE: [ ] FULL SUN [ ] PARTIAL SHADE [ ] MOSTLY SHADE [ ] FULL SHADE

WATER CROSSING: [ ] NONE [ ] ROCK HOP [ ] FOOTBRIDGE [ ] WET CROSSING

NUTRITION:

WATER: | **SNACKS:** | **MEALS:**

MAIN GEAR BROUGHT:

GEAR MISSED:

NOTES FOR NEXT TRIP:

BASICS

[ ] 1ST VISIT [ ] 2ND VISIT [ ] 3RD VISIT

DATE: /   /   LOCATION:

TRAIL:

START TIME: :   TEMP RANGE: WEATHER:
END TIME: :
DURATION: ☀ ⛅ 🌤 ☁ 🌬 ❄

COMPANIONS:

FEES: PARKING/SHUTTLES:

BRIEF RECAP OF THE EXPERIENCE:

HIKE SPECIFICS [ ] COMPLETED   [ ] NOT COMPLETED

TRAIL TYPE: [ ] LOOP   [ ] OUT & BACK [ ] POINT TO POINT

DIFFICULTY: ☆☆☆☆☆ RATING: ☆☆☆☆☆

PRIMARY TERRAIN: [ ] DIRT [ ] ROCK [ ] PAVED [ ] OTHER:

ELEVATION: GAIN/LOSS:_____ START:_____ END:_____

SUITABILITY: [ ] DOG-FRIENDLY [ ] KID-FRIENDLY [ ] STROLLER-FRIENDLY
             [ ] FULLY PAVED [ ] PARTIALLY PAVED [ ] WHEELCHAIR-FRIENDLY

TRAIL LENGTH:_____ COMPLETED: [ ] ALL [ ] OTHER: _____
TRAIL TRAFFIC: [ ] LIGHT [ ] MODERATE [ ] HEAVY
TRAIL ACTIVITIES: [ ] WALKING [ ] ROCK CLIMBING [ ] TRAIL RUNNING
                  [ ] MOUNTAIN BIKING [ ] BIRD WATCHING [ ] CAMPING
                  [ ] HORSEBACK RIDING [ ] OTHER: _____

SCENERY: [ ] NATURE VIEWS [ ] CITY VIEWS [ ] LAKE/RIVER [ ] WATERFALL
         [ ] CLIFFS [ ] FOREST [ ] HISTORIC SITE [ ] HOT SPRINGS
         [ ] WILD FLOWERS [ ] WILDLIFE [ ] OTHER: _____

EXPOSURE: [ ] NONE [ ] MINIMAL [ ] SOME [ ] EXTENSIVE

COVER/SHADE: [ ] FULL SUN [ ] PARTIAL SHADE [ ] MOSTLY SHADE [ ] FULL SHAD

WATER CROSSING: [ ] NONE [ ] ROCK HOP [ ] FOOTBRIDGE [ ] WET CROSSING

NUTRITION:

WATER: | **SNACKS:** | **MEALS:**

MAIN GEAR BROUGHT:

GEAR MISSED:

NOTES FOR NEXT TRIP:

BASICS

[ ] 1ST VISIT [ ] 2ND VISIT [ ] 3RD VISIT

DATE: /   /   LOCATION:

TRAIL:

START TIME: :   TEMP RANGE: WEATHER:
END TIME: :
DURATION: ☀ ⛅ 🌦 🌧 💨 ❄

COMPANIONS:

FEES: PARKING/SHUTTLES:

BRIEF RECAP OF THE EXPERIENCE:

HIKE SPECIFICS [ ] COMPLETED   [ ] NOT COMPLETED

TRAIL TYPE: [ ] LOOP   [ ] OUT & BACK   [ ] POINT TO POINT

DIFFICULTY: ☆☆☆☆☆ RATING: ☆☆☆☆☆

PRIMARY TERRAIN: [ ] DIRT [ ] ROCK [ ] PAVED [ ] OTHER:

ELEVATION: GAIN/LOSS:_____ START:_____ END:_____

SUITABILITY: [ ] DOG-FRIENDLY [ ] KID-FRIENDLY [ ] STROLLER-FRIENDLY
[ ] FULLY PAVED [ ] PARTIALLY PAVED [ ] WHEELCHAIR-FRIENDLY

TRAIL LENGTH:_____ COMPLETED: [ ] ALL [ ] OTHER: _____
TRAIL TRAFFIC: [ ] LIGHT [ ] MODERATE [ ] HEAVY
TRAIL ACTIVITIES: [ ] WALKING [ ] ROCK CLIMBING [ ] TRAIL RUNNING
                  [ ] MOUNTAIN BIKING [ ] BIRD WATCHING [ ] CAMPING
                  [ ] HORSEBACK RIDING [ ] OTHER: _____

SCENERY: [ ] NATURE VIEWS [ ] CITY VIEWS [ ] LAKE/RIVER [ ] WATERFALL
         [ ] CLIFFS [ ] FOREST [ ] HISTORIC SITE [ ] HOT SPRINGS
         [ ] WILD FLOWERS [ ] WILDLIFE [ ] OTHER: _____

EXPOSURE: [ ] NONE [ ] MINIMAL [ ] SOME [ ] EXTENSIVE

COVER/SHADE: [ ] FULL SUN [ ] PARTIAL SHADE [ ] MOSTLY SHADE [ ] FULL SHADE

WATER CROSSING: [ ] NONE [ ] ROCK HOP [ ] FOOTBRIDGE [ ] WET CROSSING

NUTRITION:

WATER: | **SNACKS:** | **MEALS:**

MAIN GEAR BROUGHT:

GEAR MISSED:

NOTES FOR NEXT TRIP:

BASICS

[ ] 1ST VISIT [ ] 2ND VISIT [ ] 3RD VISIT

DATE: /   /   LOCATION:

TRAIL:

START TIME: :	TEMP RANGE:	WEATHER:
END TIME: :		☼ ⛅ ⛅ 🌧 🌬 ❄
DURATION:		

COMPANIONS:

FEES: PARKING/SHUTTLES:

BRIEF RECAP OF THE EXPERIENCE:

HIKE SPECIFICS [ ] COMPLETED   [ ] NOT COMPLETED

TRAIL TYPE: [ ] LOOP   [ ] OUT & BACK   [ ] POINT TO POINT

DIFFICULTY: ☆☆☆☆☆ RATING: ☆☆☆☆☆

PRIMARY TERRAIN: [ ] DIRT [ ] ROCK [ ] PAVED [ ] OTHER:

ELEVATION: GAIN/LOSS:_____ START:_____ END:_____

SUITABILITY: [ ] DOG-FRIENDLY [ ] KID-FRIENDLY [ ] STROLLER-FRIENDLY
             [ ] FULLY PAVED [ ] PARTIALLY PAVED [ ] WHEELCHAIR-FRIENDLY

TRAIL LENGTH:_____ COMPLETED: [ ] ALL [ ] OTHER: _____
TRAIL TRAFFIC: [ ] LIGHT [ ] MODERATE [ ] HEAVY
TRAIL ACTIVITIES: [ ] WALKING [ ] ROCK CLIMBING [ ] TRAIL RUNNING
                  [ ] MOUNTAIN BIKING [ ] BIRD WATCHING [ ] CAMPING
                  [ ] HORSEBACK RIDING [ ] OTHER: _____

SCENERY: [ ] NATURE VIEWS [ ] CITY VIEWS [ ] LAKE/RIVER [ ] WATERFALL
         [ ] CLIFFS [ ] FOREST [ ] HISTORIC SITE [ ] HOT SPRINGS
         [ ] WILD FLOWERS [ ] WILDLIFE [ ] OTHER: _____

EXPOSURE: [ ] NONE [ ] MINIMAL [ ] SOME [ ] EXTENSIVE

COVER/SHADE: [ ] FULL SUN [ ] PARTIAL SHADE [ ] MOSTLY SHADE [ ] FULL SHADE

WATER CROSSING: [ ] NONE [ ] ROCK HOP [ ] FOOTBRIDGE [ ] WET CROSSING

NUTRITION:

WATER: | **SNACKS:** | **MEALS:**

MAIN GEAR BROUGHT:

GEAR MISSED:

NOTES FOR NEXT TRIP:

BASICS

[ ] 1ST VISIT [ ] 2ND VISIT [ ] 3RD VISIT

DATE: /   /   LOCATION:

TRAIL:

START TIME: :	TEMP RANGE:	WEATHER:
END TIME: :		☀ ⛅ 🌦 ☁ 🌬 ❄
DURATION:		

COMPANIONS:

FEES: PARKING/SHUTTLES:

BRIEF RECAP OF THE EXPERIENCE:

HIKE SPECIFICS [ ] COMPLETED   [ ] NOT COMPLETED

TRAIL TYPE: [ ] LOOP   [ ] OUT & BACK   [ ] POINT TO POINT

DIFFICULTY: ☆☆☆☆☆ RATING: ☆☆☆☆☆

PRIMARY TERRAIN: [ ] DIRT [ ] ROCK [ ] PAVED [ ] OTHER:

ELEVATION: GAIN/LOSS:_____ START:_____ END:_____

SUITABILITY: [ ] DOG-FRIENDLY [ ] KID-FRIENDLY [ ] STROLLER-FRIENDLY
[ ] FULLY PAVED [ ] PARTIALLY PAVED [ ] WHEELCHAIR-FRIENDLY

TRAIL LENGTH:_____ COMPLETED: [ ] ALL [ ] OTHER: _____
TRAIL TRAFFIC: [ ] LIGHT [ ] MODERATE [ ] HEAVY
TRAIL ACTIVITIES: [ ] WALKING [ ] ROCK CLIMBING [ ] TRAIL RUNNING
[ ] MOUNTAIN BIKING [ ] BIRD WATCHING [ ] CAMPING
[ ] HORSEBACK RIDING [ ] OTHER: _____

SCENERY: [ ] NATURE VIEWS [ ] CITY VIEWS [ ] LAKE/RIVER [ ] WATERFALL
[ ] CLIFFS [ ] FOREST [ ] HISTORIC SITE [ ] HOT SPRINGS
[ ] WILD FLOWERS [ ] WILDLIFE [ ] OTHER: _____

EXPOSURE: [ ] NONE [ ] MINIMAL [ ] SOME [ ] EXTENSIVE

COVER/SHADE: [ ] FULL SUN [ ] PARTIAL SHADE [ ] MOSTLY SHADE [ ] FULL SHAD

WATER CROSSING: [ ] NONE [ ] ROCK HOP [ ] FOOTBRIDGE [ ] WET CROSSING

NUTRITION:

WATER: | **SNACKS:** | **MEALS:**

MAIN GEAR BROUGHT:

GEAR MISSED:

NOTES FOR NEXT TRIP:

BASICS

[ ] 1ST VISIT [ ] 2ND VISIT [ ] 3RD VISIT

DATE: /   /   LOCATION:

TRAIL:

START TIME: :	TEMP RANGE:	WEATHER:
END TIME: :		☀ ⛅ ⛈ 🌧 💨 ❄
DURATION:		

COMPANIONS:

FEES: PARKING/SHUTTLES:

BRIEF RECAP OF THE EXPERIENCE:

HIKE SPECIFICS [ ] COMPLETED   [ ] NOT COMPLETED

TRAIL TYPE: [ ] LOOP   [ ] OUT & BACK   [ ] POINT TO POINT

DIFFICULTY: ☆☆☆☆☆ RATING: ☆☆☆☆☆

PRIMARY TERRAIN:[ ] DIRT [ ] ROCK [ ] PAVED [ ] OTHER:

ELEVATION: GAIN/LOSS:_____ START:_____ END:_____

SUITABILITY: [ ] DOG-FRIENDLY [ ] KID-FRIENDLY [ ] STROLLER-FRIENDLY
[ ] FULLY PAVED [ ] PARTIALLY PAVED [ ] WHEELCHAIR-FRIENDLY

TRAIL LENGTH:_____ COMPLETED: [ ] ALL [ ] OTHER: _____
TRAIL TRAFFIC: [ ] LIGHT [ ] MODERATE [ ] HEAVY
TRAIL ACTIVITIES: [ ] WALKING [ ] ROCK CLIMBING [ ] TRAIL RUNNING
[ ] MOUNTAIN BIKING [ ] BIRD WATCHING [ ] CAMPING
[ ] HORSEBACK RIDING [ ] OTHER: _____

SCENERY: [ ] NATURE VIEWS [ ] CITY VIEWS [ ] LAKE/RIVER [ ] WATERFALL
[ ] CLIFFS [ ] FOREST [ ] HISTORIC SITE [ ] HOT SPRINGS
[ ] WILD FLOWERS [ ] WILDLIFE [ ] OTHER: _____

EXPOSURE: [ ] NONE [ ] MINIMAL [ ] SOME [ ] EXTENSIVE

COVER/SHADE: [ ] FULL SUN [ ] PARTIAL SHADE [ ] MOSTLY SHADE [ ] FULL SHAD

WATER CROSSING: [ ] NONE [ ] ROCK HOP [ ] FOOTBRIDGE [ ] WET CROSSING

NUTRITION:

WATER: | **SNACKS:** | **MEALS:**

MAIN GEAR BROUGHT:

GEAR MISSED:

NOTES FOR NEXT TRIP:

BASICS

[ ] 1ST VISIT [ ] 2ND VISIT [ ] 3RD VISIT

DATE: /   /   LOCATION:

TRAIL:

START TIME: :   TEMP RANGE: WEATHER:
END TIME: :
DURATION:

COMPANIONS:

FEES: PARKING/SHUTTLES:

BRIEF RECAP OF THE EXPERIENCE:

HIKE SPECIFICS [ ] COMPLETED   [ ] NOT COMPLETED

TRAIL TYPE: [ ] LOOP   [ ] OUT & BACK [ ] POINT TO POINT

DIFFICULTY: ☆☆☆☆☆ RATING: ☆☆☆☆☆

PRIMARY TERRAIN:[ ] DIRT [ ] ROCK [ ] PAVED [ ] OTHER:

ELEVATION: GAIN/LOSS:_____ START:_____ END:_____

SUITABILITY:[ ] DOG-FRIENDLY [ ] KID-FRIENDLY [ ] STROLLER-FRIENDLY
           [ ] FULLY PAVED [ ] PARTIALLY PAVED [ ] WHEELCHAIR-FRIENDLY

TRAIL LENGTH:_____ COMPLETED: [ ] ALL [ ] OTHER: _____
TRAIL TRAFFIC: [ ] LIGHT [ ] MODERATE [ ] HEAVY
TRAIL ACTIVITIES: [ ] WALKING [ ] ROCK CLIMBING [ ] TRAIL RUNNING
                [ ] MOUNTAIN BIKING [ ] BIRD WATCHING [ ] CAMPING
                [ ] HORSEBACK RIDING [ ] OTHER: _____

SCENERY: [ ] NATURE VIEWS [ ] CITY VIEWS [ ] LAKE/RIVER [ ] WATERFALL
        [ ] CLIFFS [ ] FOREST [ ] HISTORIC SITE [ ] HOT SPRINGS
        [ ] WILD FLOWERS [ ] WILDLIFE [ ] OTHER: _____

EXPOSURE:[ ] NONE [ ] MINIMAL [ ] SOME [ ] EXTENSIVE

COVER/SHADE:[ ] FULL SUN [ ] PARTIAL SHADE [ ] MOSTLY SHADE [ ] FULL SHADE

WATER CROSSING:[ ] NONE [ ] ROCK HOP [ ] FOOTBRIDGE [ ] WET CROSSING

NUTRITION:

WATER: | **SNACKS:** | **MEALS:**

MAIN GEAR BROUGHT:

GEAR MISSED:

NOTES FOR NEXT TRIP:

BASICS

[ ] 1ST VISIT [ ] 2ND VISIT [ ] 3RD VISIT

DATE: / / LOCATION:

TRAIL:

START TIME: : | TEMP RANGE: | WEATHER:
END TIME: :
DURATION:

COMPANIONS:

FEES: PARKING/SHUTTLES:

BRIEF RECAP OF THE EXPERIENCE:

HIKE SPECIFICS [ ] COMPLETED [ ] NOT COMPLETED

TRAIL TYPE: [ ] LOOP [ ] OUT & BACK [ ] POINT TO POINT

DIFFICULTY: ☆☆☆☆☆ RATING: ☆☆☆☆☆

PRIMARY TERRAIN: [ ] DIRT [ ] ROCK [ ] PAVED [ ] OTHER:

ELEVATION: GAIN/LOSS:_____ START:_____ END:_____

SUITABILITY: [ ] DOG-FRIENDLY [ ] KID-FRIENDLY [ ] STROLLER-FRIENDLY
[ ] FULLY PAVED [ ] PARTIALLY PAVED [ ] WHEELCHAIR-FRIENDLY

TRAIL LENGTH:_____ COMPLETED: [ ] ALL [ ] OTHER: _____
TRAIL TRAFFIC: [ ] LIGHT [ ] MODERATE [ ] HEAVY
TRAIL ACTIVITIES: [ ] WALKING [ ] ROCK CLIMBING [ ] TRAIL RUNNING
[ ] MOUNTAIN BIKING [ ] BIRD WATCHING [ ] CAMPING
[ ] HORSEBACK RIDING [ ] OTHER: _____

SCENERY: [ ] NATURE VIEWS [ ] CITY VIEWS [ ] LAKE/RIVER [ ] WATERFALL
[ ] CLIFFS [ ] FOREST [ ] HISTORIC SITE [ ] HOT SPRINGS
[ ] WILD FLOWERS [ ] WILDLIFE [ ] OTHER: _____

EXPOSURE: [ ] NONE [ ] MINIMAL [ ] SOME [ ] EXTENSIVE

COVER/SHADE: [ ] FULL SUN [ ] PARTIAL SHADE [ ] MOSTLY SHADE [ ] FULL SHAD

WATER CROSSING: [ ] NONE [ ] ROCK HOP [ ] FOOTBRIDGE [ ] WET CROSSING

NUTRITION:

WATER: | **SNACKS:** | **MEALS:**

MAIN GEAR BROUGHT:

GEAR MISSED:

NOTES FOR NEXT TRIP:

BASICS

[ ] 1ST VISIT [ ] 2ND VISIT [ ] 3RD VISIT

DATE: /   /   LOCATION:

TRAIL:

START TIME: :   TEMP RANGE: WEATHER:
END TIME: :
DURATION:

COMPANIONS:

FEES: PARKING/SHUTTLES:

BRIEF RECAP OF THE EXPERIENCE:

HIKE SPECIFICS [ ] COMPLETED   [ ] NOT COMPLETED

TRAIL TYPE: [ ] LOOP   [ ] OUT & BACK   [ ] POINT TO POINT

DIFFICULTY: ☆☆☆☆☆   RATING: ☆☆☆☆☆

PRIMARY TERRAIN: [ ] DIRT [ ] ROCK [ ] PAVED [ ] OTHER:

ELEVATION: GAIN/LOSS:_____ START:_____ END:_____

SUITABILITY: [ ] DOG-FRIENDLY [ ] KID-FRIENDLY [ ] STROLLER-FRIENDLY
             [ ] FULLY PAVED [ ] PARTIALLY PAVED [ ] WHEELCHAIR-FRIENDLY

TRAIL LENGTH:_____ COMPLETED: [ ] ALL [ ] OTHER: _____
TRAIL TRAFFIC: [ ] LIGHT [ ] MODERATE [ ] HEAVY
TRAIL ACTIVITIES: [ ] WALKING [ ] ROCK CLIMBING [ ] TRAIL RUNNING
                  [ ] MOUNTAIN BIKING [ ] BIRD WATCHING [ ] CAMPING
                  [ ] HORSEBACK RIDING [ ] OTHER: _____

SCENERY: [ ] NATURE VIEWS [ ] CITY VIEWS [ ] LAKE/RIVER [ ] WATERFALL
         [ ] CLIFFS [ ] FOREST [ ] HISTORIC SITE [ ] HOT SPRINGS
         [ ] WILD FLOWERS [ ] WILDLIFE [ ] OTHER: _____

EXPOSURE: [ ] NONE [ ] MINIMAL [ ] SOME [ ] EXTENSIVE

COVER/SHADE: [ ] FULL SUN [ ] PARTIAL SHADE [ ] MOSTLY SHADE [ ] FULL SHADE

WATER CROSSING: [ ] NONE [ ] ROCK HOP [ ] FOOTBRIDGE [ ] WET CROSSING

NUTRITION:

WATER:	SNACKS:	MEALS:

MAIN GEAR BROUGHT:

GEAR MISSED:

NOTES FOR NEXT TRIP:

BASICS

[ ] 1ST VISIT [ ] 2ND VISIT [ ] 3RD VISIT

DATE: /   /   LOCATION:

TRAIL:

START TIME: : | TEMP RANGE: | WEATHER:
END TIME: : | | ☼ ☼ ☼ ☁ ≋ ☁
DURATION: | |

COMPANIONS:

FEES: PARKING/SHUTTLES:

BRIEF RECAP OF THE EXPERIENCE:

HIKE SPECIFICS [ ] COMPLETED   [ ] NOT COMPLETED

TRAIL TYPE: [ ] LOOP   [ ] OUT & BACK   [ ] POINT TO POINT

DIFFICULTY: ☆☆☆☆☆ RATING: ☆☆☆☆☆

PRIMARY TERRAIN: [ ] DIRT [ ] ROCK [ ] PAVED [ ] OTHER:

ELEVATION: GAIN/LOSS:_____ START:_____ END:_____

SUITABILITY: [ ] DOG-FRIENDLY [ ] KID-FRIENDLY [ ] STROLLER-FRIENDLY
             [ ] FULLY PAVED [ ] PARTIALLY PAVED [ ] WHEELCHAIR-FRIENDLY

TRAIL LENGTH:_____ COMPLETED: [ ] ALL [ ] OTHER: _____
TRAIL TRAFFIC: [ ] LIGHT [ ] MODERATE [ ] HEAVY
TRAIL ACTIVITIES: [ ] WALKING [ ] ROCK CLIMBING [ ] TRAIL RUNNING
                  [ ] MOUNTAIN BIKING [ ] BIRD WATCHING [ ] CAMPING
                  [ ] HORSEBACK RIDING [ ] OTHER: _____

SCENERY: [ ] NATURE VIEWS [ ] CITY VIEWS [ ] LAKE/RIVER [ ] WATERFALL
         [ ] CLIFFS [ ] FOREST [ ] HISTORIC SITE [ ] HOT SPRINGS
         [ ] WILD FLOWERS [ ] WILDLIFE [ ] OTHER: _____

EXPOSURE: [ ] NONE [ ] MINIMAL [ ] SOME [ ] EXTENSIVE

COVER/SHADE: [ ] FULL SUN [ ] PARTIAL SHADE [ ] MOSTLY SHADE [ ] FULL SHADE

WATER CROSSING: [ ] NONE [ ] ROCK HOP [ ] FOOTBRIDGE [ ] WET CROSSING

NUTRITION:

WATER: | **SNACKS:** | **MEALS:**

MAIN GEAR BROUGHT:

GEAR MISSED:

NOTES FOR NEXT TRIP:

BASICS

[ ] 1ST VISIT [ ] 2ND VISIT [ ] 3RD VISIT

DATE: / /   LOCATION:

TRAIL:

START TIME: :   TEMP RANGE: WEATHER:
END TIME: :
DURATION:

COMPANIONS:

FEES: PARKING/SHUTTLES:

BRIEF RECAP OF THE EXPERIENCE:

HIKE SPECIFICS [ ] COMPLETED   [ ] NOT COMPLETED

TRAIL TYPE: [ ] LOOP   [ ] OUT & BACK   [ ] POINT TO POINT

DIFFICULTY: ☆☆☆☆☆ RATING: ☆☆☆☆☆

PRIMARY TERRAIN: [ ] DIRT [ ] ROCK [ ] PAVED [ ] OTHER:

ELEVATION: GAIN/LOSS:_____ START:_____ END:_____

SUITABILITY: [ ] DOG-FRIENDLY [ ] KID-FRIENDLY [ ] STROLLER-FRIENDLY
             [ ] FULLY PAVED [ ] PARTIALLY PAVED [ ] WHEELCHAIR-FRIENDLY

TRAIL LENGTH:_____ COMPLETED: [ ] ALL [ ] OTHER: _____
TRAIL TRAFFIC: [ ] LIGHT [ ] MODERATE [ ] HEAVY
TRAIL ACTIVITIES: [ ] WALKING [ ] ROCK CLIMBING [ ] TRAIL RUNNING
                  [ ] MOUNTAIN BIKING [ ] BIRD WATCHING [ ] CAMPING
                  [ ] HORSEBACK RIDING [ ] OTHER: _____

SCENERY: [ ] NATURE VIEWS [ ] CITY VIEWS [ ] LAKE/RIVER [ ] WATERFALL
         [ ] CLIFFS [ ] FOREST [ ] HISTORIC SITE [ ] HOT SPRINGS
         [ ] WILD FLOWERS [ ] WILDLIFE [ ] OTHER: _____

EXPOSURE: [ ] NONE [ ] MINIMAL [ ] SOME [ ] EXTENSIVE

COVER/SHADE: [ ] FULL SUN [ ] PARTIAL SHADE [ ] MOSTLY SHADE [ ] FULL SHAD

WATER CROSSING: [ ] NONE [ ] ROCK HOP [ ] FOOTBRIDGE [ ] WET CROSSING

NUTRITION:

WATER: | **SNACKS:** | **MEALS:**

MAIN GEAR BROUGHT:

GEAR MISSED:

NOTES FOR NEXT TRIP:

BASICS

[ ] 1ST VISIT   [ ] 2ND VISIT   [ ] 3RD VISIT

DATE: /   /   LOCATION:

TRAIL:

START TIME: : | TEMP RANGE: | WEATHER:
END TIME: : | ☀ 🌤 ⛅ ☁ 🌬 ❄
DURATION:

COMPANIONS:

FEES: PARKING/SHUTTLES:

BRIEF RECAP OF THE EXPERIENCE:

HIKE SPECIFICS   [ ] COMPLETED   [ ] NOT COMPLETED

TRAIL TYPE: [ ] LOOP   [ ] OUT & BACK   [ ] POINT TO POINT

DIFFICULTY: ☆☆☆☆☆   RATING: ☆☆☆☆☆

PRIMARY TERRAIN: [ ] DIRT [ ] ROCK [ ] PAVED [ ] OTHER:

ELEVATION: GAIN/LOSS:_____   START:_____ END:_____

SUITABILITY: [ ] DOG-FRIENDLY [ ] KID-FRIENDLY [ ] STROLLER-FRIENDLY
             [ ] FULLY PAVED [ ] PARTIALLY PAVED [ ] WHEELCHAIR-FRIENDLY

TRAIL LENGTH:_____ COMPLETED: [ ] ALL [ ] OTHER: _____
TRAIL TRAFFIC: [ ] LIGHT [ ] MODERATE [ ] HEAVY
TRAIL ACTIVITIES: [ ] WALKING [ ] ROCK CLIMBING [ ] TRAIL RUNNING
                  [ ] MOUNTAIN BIKING [ ] BIRD WATCHING [ ] CAMPING
                  [ ] HORSEBACK RIDING [ ] OTHER: _____

SCENERY: [ ] NATURE VIEWS [ ] CITY VIEWS [ ] LAKE/RIVER [ ] WATERFALL
         [ ] CLIFFS [ ] FOREST [ ] HISTORIC SITE [ ] HOT SPRINGS
         [ ] WILD FLOWERS [ ] WILDLIFE [ ] OTHER: _____

EXPOSURE: [ ] NONE [ ] MINIMAL [ ] SOME [ ] EXTENSIVE

COVER/SHADE: [ ] FULL SUN [ ] PARTIAL SHADE [ ] MOSTLY SHADE [ ] FULL SHADE

WATER CROSSING: [ ] NONE [ ] ROCK HOP [ ] FOOTBRIDGE [ ] WET CROSSING

NUTRITION:

WATER: | **SNACKS:** | **MEALS:**

MAIN GEAR BROUGHT:

GEAR MISSED:

NOTES FOR NEXT TRIP:

BASICS

[ ] 1ST VISIT [ ] 2ND VISIT [ ] 3RD VISIT

DATE: / / LOCATION:

TRAIL:

START TIME: :	TEMP RANGE:	WEATHER:
END TIME: :		☀ ⛅ 🌦 ☁ 🌬 ❄
DURATION:		

COMPANIONS:

FEES: PARKING/SHUTTLES:

BRIEF RECAP OF THE EXPERIENCE:

HIKE SPECIFICS [ ] COMPLETED   [ ] NOT COMPLETED

TRAIL TYPE: [ ] LOOP   [ ] OUT & BACK   [ ] POINT TO POINT

DIFFICULTY: ☆☆☆☆☆ RATING: ☆☆☆☆☆

PRIMARY TERRAIN: [ ] DIRT [ ] ROCK [ ] PAVED [ ] OTHER:

ELEVATION: GAIN/LOSS:_____ START:_____ END:_____

SUITABILITY: [ ] DOG-FRIENDLY [ ] KID-FRIENDLY [ ] STROLLER-FRIENDLY
[ ] FULLY PAVED [ ] PARTIALLY PAVED [ ] WHEELCHAIR-FRIENDLY

TRAIL LENGTH:_____ COMPLETED: [ ] ALL [ ] OTHER: _____
TRAIL TRAFFIC: [ ] LIGHT [ ] MODERATE [ ] HEAVY
TRAIL ACTIVITIES: [ ] WALKING [ ] ROCK CLIMBING [ ] TRAIL RUNNING
[ ] MOUNTAIN BIKING [ ] BIRD WATCHING [ ] CAMPING
[ ] HORSEBACK RIDING [ ] OTHER: _____

SCENERY: [ ] NATURE VIEWS [ ] CITY VIEWS [ ] LAKE/RIVER [ ] WATERFALL
[ ] CLIFFS [ ] FOREST [ ] HISTORIC SITE [ ] HOT SPRINGS
[ ] WILD FLOWERS [ ] WILDLIFE [ ] OTHER: _____

EXPOSURE: [ ] NONE [ ] MINIMAL [ ] SOME [ ] EXTENSIVE

COVER/SHADE: [ ] FULL SUN [ ] PARTIAL SHADE [ ] MOSTLY SHADE [ ] FULL SHADE

WATER CROSSING: [ ] NONE [ ] ROCK HOP [ ] FOOTBRIDGE [ ] WET CROSSING

NUTRITION:

WATER:	SNACKS:	MEALS:

MAIN GEAR BROUGHT:

GEAR MISSED:

NOTES FOR NEXT TRIP:

BASICS

[ ] 1ST VISIT [ ] 2ND VISIT [ ] 3RD VISIT

DATE: /   /   LOCATION:

TRAIL:

START TIME: :   TEMP RANGE: WEATHER:
END TIME: :
DURATION:

COMPANIONS:

FEES: PARKING/SHUTTLES:

BRIEF RECAP OF THE EXPERIENCE:

HIKE SPECIFICS [ ] COMPLETED   [ ] NOT COMPLETED

TRAIL TYPE: [ ] LOOP   [ ] OUT & BACK [ ] POINT TO POINT

DIFFICULTY: ☆☆☆☆☆ RATING: ☆☆☆☆☆

PRIMARY TERRAIN: [ ] DIRT [ ] ROCK [ ] PAVED [ ] OTHER:

ELEVATION: GAIN/LOSS:_____ START:_____ END:_____

SUITABILITY: [ ] DOG-FRIENDLY [ ] KID-FRIENDLY [ ] STROLLER-FRIENDLY
             [ ] FULLY PAVED [ ] PARTIALLY PAVED [ ] WHEELCHAIR-FRIENDLY

TRAIL LENGTH:_____ COMPLETED: [ ] ALL [ ] OTHER: _____
TRAIL TRAFFIC: [ ] LIGHT [ ] MODERATE [ ] HEAVY
TRAIL ACTIVITIES: [ ] WALKING [ ] ROCK CLIMBING [ ] TRAIL RUNNING
                  [ ] MOUNTAIN BIKING [ ] BIRD WATCHING [ ] CAMPING
                  [ ] HORSEBACK RIDING [ ] OTHER: _____

SCENERY: [ ] NATURE VIEWS [ ] CITY VIEWS [ ] LAKE/RIVER [ ] WATERFALL
         [ ] CLIFFS [ ] FOREST [ ] HISTORIC SITE [ ] HOT SPRINGS
         [ ] WILD FLOWERS [ ] WILDLIFE [ ] OTHER: _____

EXPOSURE: [ ] NONE [ ] MINIMAL [ ] SOME [ ] EXTENSIVE

COVER/SHADE: [ ] FULL SUN [ ] PARTIAL SHADE [ ] MOSTLY SHADE [ ] FULL SHAD

WATER CROSSING: [ ] NONE [ ] ROCK HOP [ ] FOOTBRIDGE [ ] WET CROSSING

NUTRITION:

WATER:	SNACKS:	MEALS:

MAIN GEAR BROUGHT:

GEAR MISSED:

NOTES FOR NEXT TRIP:

BASICS

[ ] 1ST VISIT [ ] 2ND VISIT [ ] 3RD VISIT

DATE: / /   LOCATION:

TRAIL:

START TIME: :
END TIME: :
DURATION:

TEMP RANGE:

WEATHER:

☀ ⛅ 🌦 🌧 💨 ❄

COMPANIONS:

FEES: PARKING/SHUTTLES:

BRIEF RECAP OF THE EXPERIENCE:

HIKE SPECIFICS [ ] COMPLETED   [ ] NOT COMPLETED

TRAIL TYPE: [ ] LOOP   [ ] OUT & BACK   [ ] POINT TO POINT

DIFFICULTY: ☆☆☆☆☆ RATING: ☆☆☆☆☆

PRIMARY TERRAIN: [ ] DIRT [ ] ROCK [ ] PAVED [ ] OTHER:

ELEVATION: GAIN/LOSS:_____ START:_____ END:_____

SUITABILITY: [ ] DOG-FRIENDLY [ ] KID-FRIENDLY [ ] STROLLER-FRIENDLY
[ ] FULLY PAVED [ ] PARTIALLY PAVED [ ] WHEELCHAIR-FRIENDLY

TRAIL LENGTH:_____ COMPLETED: [ ] ALL [ ] OTHER: _____
TRAIL TRAFFIC: [ ] LIGHT [ ] MODERATE [ ] HEAVY
TRAIL ACTIVITIES: [ ] WALKING [ ] ROCK CLIMBING [ ] TRAIL RUNNING
[ ] MOUNTAIN BIKING [ ] BIRD WATCHING [ ] CAMPING
[ ] HORSEBACK RIDING [ ] OTHER: _____

SCENERY: [ ] NATURE VIEWS [ ] CITY VIEWS [ ] LAKE/RIVER [ ] WATERFALL
[ ] CLIFFS [ ] FOREST [ ] HISTORIC SITE [ ] HOT SPRINGS
[ ] WILD FLOWERS [ ] WILDLIFE [ ] OTHER: _____

EXPOSURE: [ ] NONE [ ] MINIMAL [ ] SOME [ ] EXTENSIVE

COVER/SHADE: [ ] FULL SUN [ ] PARTIAL SHADE [ ] MOSTLY SHADE [ ] FULL SHADE

WATER CROSSING: [ ] NONE [ ] ROCK HOP [ ] FOOTBRIDGE [ ] WET CROSSING

NUTRITION:

WATER: | **SNACKS:** | **MEALS:**

MAIN GEAR BROUGHT:

GEAR MISSED:

NOTES FOR NEXT TRIP:

BASICS

[ ] 1ST VISIT [ ] 2ND VISIT [ ] 3RD VISIT

DATE: /   /   LOCATION:

TRAIL:

START TIME: :
END TIME: :
DURATION:

TEMP RANGE:

WEATHER:
☼ ☼ ☼ ☁ 〰 ☁

COMPANIONS:

FEES: PARKING/SHUTTLES:

BRIEF RECAP OF THE EXPERIENCE:

HIKE SPECIFICS [ ] COMPLETED   [ ] NOT COMPLETED

TRAIL TYPE: [ ] LOOP   [ ] OUT & BACK   [ ] POINT TO POINT

DIFFICULTY: ☆☆☆☆☆ RATING: ☆☆☆☆☆

PRIMARY TERRAIN: [ ] DIRT [ ] ROCK [ ] PAVED [ ] OTHER:

ELEVATION: GAIN/LOSS:_____ START:_____ END:_____

SUITABILITY: [ ] DOG-FRIENDLY [ ] KID-FRIENDLY [ ] STROLLER-FRIENDLY
             [ ] FULLY PAVED [ ] PARTIALLY PAVED [ ] WHEELCHAIR-FRIENDLY

TRAIL LENGTH:_____ COMPLETED: [ ] ALL [ ] OTHER: _____
TRAIL TRAFFIC: [ ] LIGHT [ ] MODERATE [ ] HEAVY
TRAIL ACTIVITIES: [ ] WALKING [ ] ROCK CLIMBING [ ] TRAIL RUNNING
                  [ ] MOUNTAIN BIKING [ ] BIRD WATCHING [ ] CAMPING
                  [ ] HORSEBACK RIDING [ ] OTHER: _____

SCENERY: [ ] NATURE VIEWS [ ] CITY VIEWS [ ] LAKE/RIVER [ ] WATERFALL
         [ ] CLIFFS [ ] FOREST [ ] HISTORIC SITE [ ] HOT SPRINGS
         [ ] WILD FLOWERS [ ] WILDLIFE [ ] OTHER: _____

EXPOSURE: [ ] NONE [ ] MINIMAL [ ] SOME [ ] EXTENSIVE

COVER/SHADE: [ ] FULL SUN [ ] PARTIAL SHADE [ ] MOSTLY SHADE [ ] FULL SHADE

WATER CROSSING: [ ] NONE [ ] ROCK HOP [ ] FOOTBRIDGE [ ] WET CROSSING

NUTRITION:

WATER: | **SNACKS:** | **MEALS:**

MAIN GEAR BROUGHT:

GEAR MISSED:

NOTES FOR NEXT TRIP:

BASICS

[ ] 1ST VISIT [ ] 2ND VISIT [ ] 3RD VISIT

DATE: / / LOCATION:

TRAIL:

START TIME: :
END TIME: :
DURATION:

TEMP RANGE:

WEATHER:
☀ ⛅ ⛅ ☁ 🌬 ❄

COMPANIONS:

FEES: PARKING/SHUTTLES:

BRIEF RECAP OF THE EXPERIENCE:

HIKE SPECIFICS [ ] COMPLETED [ ] NOT COMPLETED

TRAIL TYPE: [ ] LOOP [ ] OUT & BACK [ ] POINT TO POINT

DIFFICULTY: ☆☆☆☆☆ **RATING:** ☆☆☆☆☆

PRIMARY TERRAIN: [ ] DIRT [ ] ROCK [ ] PAVED [ ] OTHER:

ELEVATION: GAIN/LOSS:_____ START:_____ END:_____

SUITABILITY: [ ] DOG-FRIENDLY [ ] KID-FRIENDLY [ ] STROLLER-FRIENDLY
[ ] FULLY PAVED [ ] PARTIALLY PAVED [ ] WHEELCHAIR-FRIENDLY

TRAIL LENGTH:_____ COMPLETED: [ ] ALL [ ] OTHER: _____
TRAIL TRAFFIC: [ ] LIGHT [ ] MODERATE [ ] HEAVY
TRAIL ACTIVITIES: [ ] WALKING [ ] ROCK CLIMBING [ ] TRAIL RUNNING
[ ] MOUNTAIN BIKING [ ] BIRD WATCHING [ ] CAMPING
[ ] HORSEBACK RIDING [ ] OTHER: _____

SCENERY: [ ] NATURE VIEWS [ ] CITY VIEWS [ ] LAKE/RIVER [ ] WATERFALL
[ ] CLIFFS [ ] FOREST [ ] HISTORIC SITE [ ] HOT SPRINGS
[ ] WILD FLOWERS [ ] WILDLIFE [ ] OTHER: _____

EXPOSURE: [ ] NONE [ ] MINIMAL [ ] SOME [ ] EXTENSIVE

COVER/SHADE: [ ] FULL SUN [ ] PARTIAL SHADE [ ] MOSTLY SHADE [ ] FULL SHAD

WATER CROSSING: [ ] NONE [ ] ROCK HOP [ ] FOOTBRIDGE [ ] WET CROSSING

NUTRITION:

WATER: | **SNACKS:** | **MEALS:**

MAIN GEAR BROUGHT:

GEAR MISSED:

NOTES FOR NEXT TRIP:

BASICS

[ ] 1ST VISIT [ ] 2ND VISIT [ ] 3RD VISIT

DATE: /   /   LOCATION:

TRAIL:

START TIME: :   TEMP RANGE: WEATHER:
END TIME: :
DURATION:

COMPANIONS:

FEES: PARKING/SHUTTLES:

BRIEF RECAP OF THE EXPERIENCE:

HIKE SPECIFICS [ ] COMPLETED   [ ] NOT COMPLETED

TRAIL TYPE: [ ] LOOP   [ ] OUT & BACK   [ ] POINT TO POINT

DIFFICULTY: ☆☆☆☆☆ RATING: ☆☆☆☆☆

PRIMARY TERRAIN: [ ] DIRT [ ] ROCK [ ] PAVED [ ] OTHER:

ELEVATION: GAIN/LOSS:_____ START:_____ END:_____

SUITABILITY: [ ] DOG-FRIENDLY [ ] KID-FRIENDLY [ ] STROLLER-FRIENDLY
            [ ] FULLY PAVED [ ] PARTIALLY PAVED [ ] WHEELCHAIR-FRIENDLY

TRAIL LENGTH:_____ COMPLETED: [ ] ALL [ ] OTHER: _____
TRAIL TRAFFIC: [ ] LIGHT [ ] MODERATE [ ] HEAVY
TRAIL ACTIVITIES: [ ] WALKING [ ] ROCK CLIMBING [ ] TRAIL RUNNING
                 [ ] MOUNTAIN BIKING [ ] BIRD WATCHING [ ] CAMPING
                 [ ] HORSEBACK RIDING [ ] OTHER: _____

SCENERY: [ ] NATURE VIEWS [ ] CITY VIEWS [ ] LAKE/RIVER [ ] WATERFALL
         [ ] CLIFFS [ ] FOREST [ ] HISTORIC SITE [ ] HOT SPRINGS
         [ ] WILD FLOWERS [ ] WILDLIFE [ ] OTHER: _____

EXPOSURE: [ ] NONE [ ] MINIMAL [ ] SOME [ ] EXTENSIVE

COVER/SHADE: [ ] FULL SUN [ ] PARTIAL SHADE [ ] MOSTLY SHADE [ ] FULL SHADE

WATER CROSSING: [ ] NONE [ ] ROCK HOP [ ] FOOTBRIDGE [ ] WET CROSSING

NUTRITION:

WATER: | **SNACKS:** | **MEALS:**

MAIN GEAR BROUGHT:

GEAR MISSED:

NOTES FOR NEXT TRIP:

BASICS

[ ] 1ST VISIT [ ] 2ND VISIT [ ] 3RD VISIT

DATE: / /   LOCATION:

TRAIL:

START TIME: :	TEMP RANGE:	WEATHER:
END TIME: :		☀ ⛅ 🌦 ☁ 🌬 ❄
DURATION:		

COMPANIONS:

FEES: PARKING/SHUTTLES:

BRIEF RECAP OF THE EXPERIENCE:

HIKE SPECIFICS [ ] COMPLETED [ ] NOT COMPLETED

TRAIL TYPE: [ ] LOOP [ ] OUT & BACK [ ] POINT TO POINT

DIFFICULTY: ☆☆☆☆☆ RATING: ☆☆☆☆☆

PRIMARY TERRAIN: [ ] DIRT [ ] ROCK [ ] PAVED [ ] OTHER:

ELEVATION: GAIN/LOSS:_____ START:_____ END:_____

SUITABILITY: [ ] DOG-FRIENDLY [ ] KID-FRIENDLY [ ] STROLLER-FRIENDLY
[ ] FULLY PAVED [ ] PARTIALLY PAVED [ ] WHEELCHAIR-FRIENDLY

TRAIL LENGTH:_____ COMPLETED: [ ] ALL [ ] OTHER: _____
TRAIL TRAFFIC: [ ] LIGHT [ ] MODERATE [ ] HEAVY
TRAIL ACTIVITIES: [ ] WALKING [ ] ROCK CLIMBING [ ] TRAIL RUNNING
[ ] MOUNTAIN BIKING [ ] BIRD WATCHING [ ] CAMPING
[ ] HORSEBACK RIDING [ ] OTHER: _____

SCENERY: [ ] NATURE VIEWS [ ] CITY VIEWS [ ] LAKE/RIVER [ ] WATERFALL
[ ] CLIFFS [ ] FOREST [ ] HISTORIC SITE [ ] HOT SPRINGS
[ ] WILD FLOWERS [ ] WILDLIFE [ ] OTHER: _____

EXPOSURE: [ ] NONE [ ] MINIMAL [ ] SOME [ ] EXTENSIVE

COVER/SHADE: [ ] FULL SUN [ ] PARTIAL SHADE [ ] MOSTLY SHADE [ ] FULL SHADE

WATER CROSSING: [ ] NONE [ ] ROCK HOP [ ] FOOTBRIDGE [ ] WET CROSSING

NUTRITION:

WATER: | **SNACKS:** | **MEALS:**

MAIN GEAR BROUGHT:

GEAR MISSED:

NOTES FOR NEXT TRIP:

COMMON HIKING TERMS:

SOURCE: HARTLEY BRODY ADVENTURE BLOG (USED WITH PERMISSION)
https://adventures.hartleybrody.com/glossary-of-hiking-backpacking-terms-acronyms/

10 Essentials (or Ten Essentials)
An ever-evolving list of "essentials" that everyone should take on every hike, in case of an emergency or if they get lost and need to spend an unplanned night out. The list usually includes map and compass, sun protection (hat, sunglasses, sunscreen), extra layers, fire starting materials (lighter, matches, tinder), snacks, first aid supplies, illumination (flashlight or headlamp) and various camp tools (knife, axe, trowel). Check out my Ultimate Backpacking Checklist for a full list of overnight essentials.

100MW
The "100 Mile Wilderness" is a remote stretch of the AT in northern Maine. The 100 Mile Wilderness is known for being very remote and grueling, with limited resupply options along the way. It's on my list of best New England Hikes.

Alpine Zone
The area near the tops of tall peaks where it's too windy and the soil is too thin to allow trees or large plants to grow. The exact altitude where the alpine zone starts can vary between regions and even mountains in similar regions, due to local weather patterns. Alpine Zones are usually covered in snow fields or Talus.

AMC
The "Appalachian Mountain Club" has a huge presence in the White Mountains of New Hampshire, as well as throughout some of the more popular backcountry destinations across New England. The run a number of high-end Huts.

AT
The "Appalachian Trail," a 2,184 mile long trail between Springer Mountain in Georgia and Mount Katahdin in Maine.

Base Weight
The weight of your backpack plus all the gear that's inside it, but not counting consumables like food, water and fuel. Your Base Weight is mostly determined by your "Big 3" items: sleeping bag, backpack and shelter. Most backpackers should shoot for a Base Weight of 15-20lbs. Ultralight backpackers have a Base Weight of 10-12lbs or less.

Beta
Beta is specific, insider information about a hike, usually coming from someone who just completed it. A lot of times you can get good beta about an upcoming hike by talking to people in town or on message boards. They might tell you about specific tricky spots, shortcuts, Caches or other good-to-know information.

'biner
Short for carabiner, those metal clips that climbers use to secure rope, slings and other gear. Often used by hikers to attach things to their pack or hang things up around camp.

Bivy Sack (or Bivvy Sack)
A waterproof sack that goes over your sleeping bag to add warmth and protection from the elements. Some hikers carry them as an emergency shelter, while other hikers may use it as their primary shelter, or to add more protection and warmth to another tarp shelter.

Blaze
A colored mark, usually painted or nailed to a tree, about 4 inches tall by 2 inches wide. These are used to help guide hikers if the trail gets hard to follow or makes an abrupt turn. Some areas use color-coded systems to help hikers figure out which trail they're on.

Bluebird Day
A day marked by completely cloudless, clear blue skies. Such great weather has been known to cause a strong sense of euphoria and a hearty fist pump, especially when hiking up in Alpine Zones.

Book Time
Book Time is a reference to the estimated amount of time a hike should take, following this simple formula: 30 minutes for each mile plus 30 minutes for each 1,000 feet of elevation gain along the hike. It's the formula that the AMC and many others use to provide a ballpark estimate of a hike's duration.

Bushwhack
Bushwhacking is the process of travelling off-trail, sometimes through dense trees, branches and bushes. While trails are usually wide and clear, Bushwacking off-trail may be much slower since the hiker is required to detour around — or fight their way through — the bushes and trees in their way.

Cache
A Cache is a place where you store gear, food and other supplies before a long trip. The Cache is usually on or near the trail, allowing you to resupply when you reach it.

Cairn
A structure made of rocks used to mark a trail where trees aren't present for Blazes, like in Alpine Zones. Some are just loose piles while others are more decorative.

Camel Up
Cameling Up is a process to help you stay hydrated without needing to carry lots of heavy water bottles during your hike. When you reach a water source, you refill quickly -- usually with an inline filter like a Sawyer Mini -- and then gulp down all the water immediately before heading off down the trail again. This allows you to get the water into your system quickly while avoiding the need to carry heavy, full water bottles (~2.5

pounds per liter!) on the hike. A technique commonly used by Ultralight hikers.

Cat Hole
A small hole that you dig in order to bury poop and toilet paper. Only use Cat Holes in areas with at least 6-8" of soil and Detritus. In Alpine Zones, deserts and other areas, you may be expected to pack out your human waste in a plastic bag.

CDT
The "Continental Divide Trail," a 3,100 mile long trail, following the Continental Divide along the Rocky Mountains and traversing Montana, Idaho, Wyoming, Colorado, and New Mexico.

Col (or "Notch")
A col is the lowest point on the ridge between two peaks. Sometimes referred to as a "Notch" or "Saddle," it is the point where you stop descending one peak and start ascending the next one.

Contour Lines
Contour Lines appear on Topographic Maps and represent a line between all nearby points at the same elevation. If Contour Lines are close together in an area, that means it changes elevation quickly and is very steep. Contour lines tend to form circles around mountains (if the inner lines are higher elevation) or lakes (if the inner ones are lower elevation), and also point upstream when crossing over rivers.

Cowboy Camping
Cowboy Camping entails setting up camp the way the cowboys did out west -- under the open sky. Generally it's a sleeping bag on the ground with no tarp or tent overhead. It can be a great way to enjoy a clear, starry night, but make sure there's no rain in the forecast so you don't wake up soaking wet!

Declination (or Magnetic Declination)

Declination refers to the angle between "Magnetic North" (where your compass needle points) and "True North" (a straight line from you towards the actual North Pole). Depending on where in the world you are, these two measurements can differ by as much as 50°, so it's important to know the local Declination if you'll be taking precise bearings or doing any serious map and compass navigation.

Detritus (or Duff)

All of the leaves, pine needles, branches, sticks and other dead and decaying plant materials that cover most forest floors. In autumn when the leaves have just fallen, this can be many inches thick.

Dirtbag

An avid outdoorsman or woman who eschews the comforts of civilization in order to more fully realize their outdoor passion. Often dirty with unkempt hair & living in a vehicle, they're usually seen wearing flannel shirts & ski boots or climbing shoes.

EMS

While it might sometimes refer to "Emergency Medical Services," if someone is talking about gear that they bought at EMS, they're probably referring to "Eastern Mountain Sports," an outdoor retailer based in New England.

False Peak (or False Summit)

Depending on the shape of a mountain, you may look up the trail and think you see the peak just ahead. But once you reach that spot, you may be dismayed to see that it was just a shoulder or small bump - a False Peak - and that the real peak still likes farther up the trail.

FKT

The "Fastest Known Time" is the record for completing a section of trail (usually a Thru Hike) in the shortest possible ne. There usually isn't a single authority that tracks FKT, stead it's up to the community to verify GPS data or social edia posts the hiker made along the way to ensure the new cord is "legit," although FKT records can still be somewhat ontroversial.

ord

Ford is a river crossing that involves getting your feet wet. you anticipate a Ford on your trip, you'll usually bring andals or a change of footwear to use -- never barefoot! leally, the water won't come much higher than your knees o that there's less risk of being swept away. Make sure you ave a plan in case you lose your footing so that you and our stuff don't wash away. Trekking poles can help with tability during Fords. If the water level is very low, a Ford nay turn into a simple, quick Rock Hop.

ilissade

liding down a snow-covered field on your rear end, like ledding without the sled. A much faster (and more fun) way o descend steep snow fields, just be careful that you can ontrol your speed and direction so you don't slide into a ree or off a cliff.

iORP

raditionally, Good Old Raisins and Peanuts. Some claim 's Granola, Oats, Raisins, Peanuts. Either way, it's usually a ig bag full of salty and savory snacks that you eat by the andful.

iPS

he "Global Positioning System" is a constellation of atellites run by the US Military that powers everything from he turn-by-turn directions in your phone to the location racking in your favorite navigation device.

Herd Path
An unofficial trail that's formed when a large numbers of hikers decide to all follow a similar footpath over time, similar to how game trails are formed by animals. They're usually created as hikers take a natural shortcut or easier path around some obstacle.

Hump
To begrudgingly carry an excessively heavy load. It's often the responsibility of the guide or leader of a group to carry a ton of extra group gear that they wouldn't normally take. Climbers also often have to Hump in their entire gear rack until they get to the base of their climb.

Hut
Huts can vary from dilapidated old sheds to full-service hotels. They are a permanent backcountry shelter with four walls and roof that can sleep any number of backpackers, depending on their size.

HYOH
Meaning "Hike Your Own Hike," the idea that we should all live and let live on the trail.

JMT
The "John Muir Trail" is a 210 mile trail that follows a section of the PCT. Almost entirely above 8,000 ft of elevation, much of the trail is in the Alpine Zone, with gorgeous big-mountain views and wildflowers.

Lean-to (or Leanto)
A sturdy shelter built along popular trails that consists of a raised floor, roof and three walls. They usually fit anywhere from four to a dozen backpackers. With one wall left open, lean-tos allow you to escape wind and precipitation while still performing camp chores like cooking.

LNT (or Leave No Trace)
"Leave No Trace" is a series of 7 principles designed to help backpackers and campers think about ways to minimize the impact that their presence has on the natural environment.

MEC
"Mountain Equipment Co-op" is the largest outdoor retailer in Canada. Originally catering specifically to alpine mountaineers, they've been moving to focus on a wider audience of outdoor enthusiasts.

Monorail
Monorail is the term used to describe the narrow band of snow and ice that remains down the center of a trail into late spring, even after most of the other snow has melted. It forces hikers to either walk on it like a balance beam or else forces them into the mud on either side.

NOBO
Short for "North Bound." A term used to describe Thru Hikers that start at the southern terminus of a long trail and head north.

NOLS
The "National Outdoor Leadership School" is one of the largest and most well-known outdoor education programs. They lead trips all over the world for students and adults of all ages. The also teach a number of wilderness medicine classes like WFR through their Wilderness Medicine Institute (WMI).

NPS
The National Park Service in the United States, in charge of running and protecting the National Parks.

PCT
The "Pacific Crest Trail," a 2,654 miles long trail through Washington, Oregon, and California following the highest portion of the Sierra Nevada and Cascade Range.

Peak Bagging

The process of summiting (or "bagging") a collection of related peaks in an area. It's like going through a to-do list of challenging but rewarding hikes. Popular Peak Bagging lists include the "New Hampshire 4000 Footers" (48 peaks) and the "Colorado Fourteeners" (53 peaks).

Posthole

When hiking through fresh, deep snow, Postholing is when each step you take sinks far down into the snow, sometimes burying your entire leg. Postholing is extremely tiring and slow-going. Groups of hikers will often switch up the person in the front, allowing the old leader the easier task of following in the new leader's footsteps (or Postholes).

PUD

"Pointless Ups and Downs" are areas of annoyingly rolling terrain that don't actually result in any elevation gain. Despite some trails going up and over several 30' hills in a row, that section would appear as "flat" terrain on most Topographic Maps, causing extra frustration for any unsuspecting hikers. Knowing about PUDs ahead of time requires getting good Beta.

Redline

To have "Redlined" an area means that you've hiked every single inch of trail in it, including all of the major trails as well as all of the smaller connector sections. Print out a map of the area you want to Redline and trace all the trails you've already done with a red marker. Whatever is left uncovered is where you hike next. You've completed a Redline attempt when every section of every trail is "Redlined out". It's the ultimate measure of really knowing an area like the back of your hand.

REI

One of the most popular outdoor retailers in the US, "Recreational Equipment, Inc." is a common place for first-timers to load up on camping and hiking gear.

Rock Hop
A Rock Hop is a river or stream crossing that can be done without getting your feet wet. Generally done by hopping from rock to rock through a low-running channel of water. A Rock Hop is generally faster and safer than a Ford.

SAR
Stands for "Search and Rescue," they're almost always volunteers who leave their families and careers behind when backcountry enthusiasts get themselves into trouble.

Scree
A field of loose rocks smaller than the size of your head. It can be very tricky to keep your footing in a Scree field. The small rocks will often move or slide underfoot, making it very tricky to avoid ankle or knee injuries.

Section Hike
When someone isn't able to complete a Thru Hike in one contiguous effort, they may instead choose to complete the trail over a longer period by hiking smaller sections of it and returning to society in between. A term popularized by Phillip Werner.

Slackpacking
Carrying a minimal load of food, water and gear, usually because someone else in your group is Humping everything else, or because you're planning to stay in Huts along your route.

SOBO
Short for "South Bound." A term used to describe Thru Hikers that start at the northern terminus of a long trail and head south.

Stealth Camp (or Dispersed Camp)

To setup a low-impact campsite in a more pristine nook, away from more heavily-used campsites. It can be useful to help avoid bugs, bears, mice and other creatures that have become accustomed to campers' presence in a certain area. Stealth camping is frowned upon by many since it is hard to do well and truly Leave No Trace. In popular areas, it's better to centralize the human traffic to one area to avoid leaving marks and blemishes all over the landscape.

Switchbacks
When a trail zig-zags back-and-forth up a very steep section of terrain. It adds distance to a trail but also makes it easier to hike - think of climbing straight up a ladder versus covering the same height on a very long ramp. Switchbacks also help prevent erosion on steep slopes, so be sure to follow the trail and avoid the temptation to cut straight up.

Talus
A field of larger boulders that often requires hands and feed to scramble over. Route-finding can be very slow and laborious through Talus fields. Commonly found in Alpine Zones.

The Big Three (or The Big 3)
The three most essential pieces of gear that any backpacker carries: sleeping bag, backpack and shelter. These items also tend to be the heaviest, so those looking to go Ultralight often look to these 3 items to cut the most from their Base Weight.

Thru Hike
Hiking an entire trail contiguously from end-to-end, usually at least 100 miles over more than a week. Famous Thru Hikes include the Appalachian Trail (AT) and Pacific Crest Trail (PCT).

Thru Hiker

Someone who is in the process of completing a Thru Hike.
See also Dirtbag. LOL

Topo (or Topographic)

Topography focuses on the shape and features of the land
– hills and valleys, rivers and lakes. A topographic map
(or "Topo Map") is one that shows the natural features of a
landscape, including Contour Lines of similar elevation.

Trail Angel

A local who isn't actively hiking the trail but does nice things
for hikers who are. Trail Angels may run van shuttles from the
trailhead into town, or leave Caches of snacks or beer along
the trail.

Trail Name

Often Thru Hikers will adopt a moniker or nickname while
they're on the trail. It usually has an interesting backstory and
tends to be given by another Thru Hiker after a particularly
memorable experience. It can be a way for the Thru Hiker
to dissociate their "real" identity back home with the antics
they're up to on the trail.

Trail Magic

Trail Magic is a surprise treat or Cache left on the trail for
future hikers to enjoy. Sometimes they're intentionally left by
Trail Angels and sometimes they're lost or discarded items
that earlier hikers left behind.

Trailhead

The trailhead is the place where your hike starts or stops
-- where you cross over from being in civilization to being in
the backcountry. Most trailheads have a parking lot and many
offer free maps or signs with information about the hikes you
can access from them.

Triple Crown
The crowning accomplishment of Thru Hiking the AT, PCT. and CDT.

UL (or Ultralight)
The goal of going Ultralight is to carry a Base Weight of less than 10-12lbs. There are many reasons for going Ultralight and most of them boil down to the fact that you can hike farther, faster, and see more without getting as tired and with less chance of injury. The trade-off with carrying less gear is that you need more experience and skills (which weigh nothing).

USGS
The United States Geological Survey, an agency who produces free Topographic Maps for virtually every corner of the US.

WFA
"Wilderness First Aid" is usually a weekend-long course covering the basics of Wilderness Medicine for avid outdoorsmen and women. It covers the basics of patient assessment and how to treat and improvise solutions for basic, common medical problems.

WFR (or Woofer)
A "Wilderness First Responder" is someone who has taken a week-long class on intermediate-level Wilderness Medicine. Most mountain guides and Search and Rescue personnel are trained to Wilderness First Responder level.

Zero Day (or Take a Zero)
A zero day is when you spend two nights in a row in the same campsite and don't do any hiking during the day. This can be used on longer Thru Hikes to help recover from injury, rest, or wait out a storm.

ISBN: 9781702409865

Made in the USA
Las Vegas, NV
14 February 2024

85770436R00080